COVID-19, Familism, and South Korean Governance

This book traces the factors that contributed to the success in controlling the COVID-19 pandemic in South Korea and identifies the concept of familism as a major environmental factor.

The government of South Korea has achieved remarkable outcomes in its COVID-19 response, despite the fact that South Korea usually promotes a family-focused investment of resources at the expense of broader social goals. The author eschews these Western cultural biases in theories of crisis management and suggests that the key component of South Korea's success is not self-centered egotism of individuals but a focus on family and familism, which projects state as an extension of family. He argues that, while the success in managing the COVID-19 epidemic is due to a combination of factors, familism has been a key force in driving this successful response to the COVID-19 outbreak.

The book will be of interest to scholars and students of governance, crisis management, civil society, and citizen's participation in public administration, international relations, Asian studies, and cultural studies and Confucianism.

Dr. Jai Chang Park earned his doctorate in Public Administration from the State University of New York at Albany and is serving as a professor emeritus of the Public Administration Department at the Sookmyung Women's University in Seoul, Korea.

COVID-19, Familism, and South Korean Governance

Jai Chang Park

LONDON AND NEW YORK

First published 2022
by Routledge
2 Park Square, Milton Park, Abingdon, Oxon OX14 4RN

and by Routledge
605 Third Avenue, New York, NY 10158

Routledge is an imprint of the Taylor & Francis Group, an informa business

© 2022 Jai Chang Park

The right of Jai Chang Park to be identified as author of this work has been asserted in accordance with sections 77 and 78 of the Copyright, Designs and Patents Act 1988.

All rights reserved. No part of this book may be reprinted or reproduced or utilised in any form or by any electronic, mechanical, or other means, now known or hereafter invented, including photocopying and recording, or in any information storage or retrieval system, without permission in writing from the publishers.

Trademark notice: Product or corporate names may be trademarks or registered trademarks, and are used only for identification and explanation without intent to infringe.

British Library Cataloguing-in-Publication Data
A catalogue record for this book is available from the British Library

Library of Congress Cataloging-in-Publication Data
Names: Pak, Chae-ch'ang, 1948– author.
Title: COVID-19, familism, and South Korean governance / Jai Chang Park.
Description: First Edition. | New York : Routledge, 2022. | Includes bibliographical references and index.
Identifiers: LCCN 2021031317 (print) | LCCN 2021031318 (ebook) | ISBN 9781032147161 (Hardback) | ISBN 9781032147178 (Paperback) | ISBN 9781003240709 (eBook)
Subjects: LCSH: Crisis management in government—Korea (South) | Public administration—Korea (South)—Citizen participation. | Families—Korea (South) | Information society—Social aspects—Korea (South) | COVID-19 (Disease)—Political aspects—Korea (South) | COVID-19 (Disease)—Economic aspects—Korea (South)
Classification: LCC JQ1725.A55 .P367 2022 (print) | LCC JQ1725.A55 (ebook) | DDC 320.95195—dc23
LC record available at https://lccn.loc.gov/2021031317
LC ebook record available at https://lccn.loc.gov/2021031318

ISBN: 9781032147161 (hbk)
ISBN: 9781032147178 (pbk)
ISBN: 9781003240709 (ebk)

DOI: 10.4324/9781003240709

Typeset in Times New Roman
by Apex CoVantage, LLC

Contents

Illustrations		vii
About the author		viii
Preface: between the frustration of human civilization and the self-esteem of South Korean culture		ix

1 Introduction   1

2 Seeking crisis response implementation governance   4
    1. Spread of COVID-19 and social crisis 4
    2. Contradictory issues in crisis response strategies 7
    3. Types of crisis response implementation governance 8

3 South Korea's sociocultural characteristics and state   14
    1. Low-trust society and flat state 14
    2. Familism and dual state 19
    3. Wartime culture and switching state 25

4 South Korea's COVID-19 response implementation governance   29
    1. Overview of South Korea's COVID-19 response 29
    2. Manifestation of crisis consciousness and family state frame 31
    3. Meritocracy and contract state frame 37

5 Outcomes of COVID-19 response implementation governance   42
    1. Family state and social capital 42
    2. Switching state and contextual governance 44
    3. Dual state and cultural approach 46

4. Information society and proactive governance 48
5. Success of crisis response and overcoming
   Western cultural bias 50

6 Conclusion   53

References   57
Index   63

Illustrations

Table 2.1 Types of crisis response policy implementation governance 12

Figure 4.1 Degree of severity of crisis situation, degree of positiveness of government response, and number of new confirmers per day 30

About the author

Dr. Jai Chang Park earned his doctorate in Public Administration from the State University of New York at Albany and is serving as a professor emeritus of the Public Administration Department at the Sookmyung Women's University in Seoul, Korea. He served as President of the Korean Association for Public Administration, the Korean Association of NGO Studies, the Association of International Area Studies of Korea and the Korean Society for Politics–Administration Studies. He was Endowed Chair Professor at Hankuk University of Foreign Studies in Korea, Fulbright Scholar at UC Berkeley in the United States, Humboldt Foundation Research Professor at the Free University of Berlin in Germany, Guest Professor at Doshisha University in Japan, and Congressional Fellow of the American Political Science Association. He is the author and editor of numerous scholarly books, including *Ombudsman: The 4th Branch, Global Governance and NGOs, New Governance: Issues and Challenges, National Remodelling in Governance Era, Governance in Korea, Citizen's Participation and Governance, Global Citizenship and Social Movements, Korean Civil Society in Crisis, Government and NGOs, Global Civil Society and Korean NGOs, Korean Legislative Administration, Korean Legislative Politics, Korean Digital Legislature, Korean Legislative Reform, Korean Legislative Ethics*, and *Legislative Staff in Korea*, etc.

Preface

Between the frustration of human civilization and the self-esteem of South Korean culture

COVID-19 is a global pandemic with strong infectivity, high case fatality, and reinfection rate. Nevertheless, nothing much is known about it. Respiratory transmission is the main infection pathway, but there are still different views on which media weight is higher between the air and the droplets. The same goes for not being able to lift the veil about asymptomatic propagation, immune response, reinfection, the role of the genetic predisposition, and the long-term effects of infection. In such a situation, it is no surprise that we are in the predevelopment stage of preventive medicines and treatments. The expectation was that vaccine development would bring about a reversal of the situation. However, there are still many mountains to climb, such as variations in viruses, breakthrough infections, side effects, and achieving herd immunity. It is no different from the "crisis of medical science". As a result, the people of the global village, who are living in the most scientifically developed era in human history, are undergoing very humbling and uneasy daily lives.

In response to such circumstances, the state has the responsibility of controlling disease and protecting the health of the people. The state's fundamental rationale for existence is to protect and maintain the safety and dignity of the people. Such a state is currently at risk inasmuch as politics plays a pivotal role in any state, particularly when a severe "political crisis" arises. The pursuit of the values that are worthy of protection for any modern state conflicts with the prioritization of the individual nation's practical interests. If it is to be a civilized nation, it deserves to strive for humanitarianism, respect human rights, and work toward the well-being of the entire world as it faces one of the worst catastrophes in the history of human civilization. As the outbreak of COVID-19 is one of the derivative effects of global warming, we should work most aggressively to respond to environmental pollution and ecological destruction throughout the global village. Cooperation and collaboration among nations are essential for the effective control and prevention of COVID-19 as it spreads across borders. The supply chain of daily necessities produced in foreign countries must be maintained so that the viable economies of their peoples can be sustained even amid such a disaster. However, border closings, vaccine ultranationalism, and competitive capitalism seem to be very realistic options for a country in that they prioritize the protection of the well-being of its own people and its own businesses by adopting medical capitalism. In such a case, it is inevitable or even prescriptive for individual states to protect their interests, compete with other countries, or prioritize protecting their people through strategic and independent responses to the disease.

Even within a given country, circumstances are no different. To control infectious disease effectively, a prevention and control policy needs to be developed and implemented according to medical knowledge and scientific judgment. However, no policy can exert the expected effect without the active response and participation of the public, the policy's executors. Therefore, it needs a process of political adjustment to coordinate the preferences and interests of all citizens. It means that the monism of medical science and the pluralism of political coordination cannot but conflict with each other. This process of coordination and compromise requires time to reframe and adjust different views and vying interests. In responding to an urgent situation, it is possible to lose the appropriate timing. In the political adjustment process, managing the differences in participation capabilities and the inequalities in opportunities that arise between the socioeconomically vulnerable and the socioeconomically strong is also one of the complex tasks that government must deal with. The complexity of the problem only grows when we consider that the uneven medical impacts of COVID-19 coincide with the socioeconomic inequality of the people.

Even when the direction or content of infectious disease prevention and control policy is determined, the "administrative crisis" that arises in executing it is no easy task. This is because we cannot respond to crises through the usual forms of administration established before the COVID-19 crisis. The biggest problem is the sudden increase in the overall amount of work simply because the work of responding to the crisis is added to the day-to-day work required to conduct routine state affairs. In particular, such emergency work cannot be easily accomplished simply by following existing standard procedures or normal response modes. We cannot appropriately respond to the needs for on-site compliance, resilience, flexibility, and speed that crises demand by simply following the up-and-down working mechanisms of bureaucracy and the rule of law, with their universal, general, and rigid work procedures. However, given the urgency of the situation, it is not even possible to recruit and train additional human resources, develop new and innovative working mechanisms, and disseminate them across all of government in time. Above all, to efficiently manage administration, a systematized procedure is required to overcome the conflicting circumstances created by the judgments of the management experts on the front lines of policy delivery, the individual needs requested by the disaster control beneficiaries, and the diagnoses extended by the medical experts. In this case, we come up against the problem that actively and flexibly responding to such situational change is difficult. One of the essential problems is that it is difficult to estimate and trace cause-and-effect relationships or to develop efficient response measures as the nature of the problem itself is ambiguous and uncertain.

Therefore, real-time adjustments that are gradually made in responding to the changing situation become inevitable. It means that alternatives must be found amid a series of constant tensions and contradictions, like groping in the dark. For example, is it right to quickly disclose all disease-related information and seek citizen's buy-in and consent? Even then, wouldn't doing so cause excessive fear and anxious consciousness of the disease? For information accuracy and transparency, should we increase people's understanding and ability to use medical jargon? Or should we deliver information in general terms, even at the risk of uncertainty in content? The administration, which must come up with answers to these contradictory challenges, is forever bound by a series of tensions and torsions. More seriously, when the government's administration is perceived as if it has lost its ability to solve problems, it loses its own efficacy while increasing the risk of intensifying its own torsion, such as corruption, evasion of the law, opportunism, non-decision-making, and negligence. Differences in the perception of the nature of the crisis bring conflict and dysfunction and, further, lead to more significant problems among the stakeholders in the prevention and control of infectious disease.

A more fundamental problem is that, as the infectious disease prevention and control administration continues and becomes routinized, the defense mechanism of people against big government and state interventionism is weakened, and attitudes that take surveillance and intervention by the government for granted become a kind of social tendency. This phenomenon has already been confirmed in modern history. The routinization of big government has persisted ever since the United States justified state interventionism through the New Deal policy during the Great Depression of the 1930s, and the Marshall Plan, designed for the revival of Europe amid the ruins of World War II, expanded the social legitimacy base of the centralized response and deepening of government dependency. Similarly, the "economic crisis" caused by COVID-19 raised the needs for the expansion of the government's fiscal input as an inevitable alternative. Economic activity shrinks and economic inequality deepens among the social and economic tiers, as infectious disease prevention and control measures, such as border closures, urban blockades, social distancing, and self-quarantine, become taken for granted. Meanwhile, the beneficiaries of infectious disease prevention and control policies are universal and general. The burden of the socioeconomic cost is borne by specific and individual segments of society. The damage to the economically vulnerable, such as the self-employed, the contingent workers, and the small and medium-sized businesses, is more significant and more often fatal. To support and reward these socioeconomically vulnerable people and to sustain the economy's day-to-day operation, we cannot help but greatly expand the state's fiscal commitment, such that the advent of big government will be taken for granted. This threatens political liberalism and economic capitalism and dramatically increases the chances of populism emerging. It means that we are to face an era of "ideological crisis".

However, state intervention alone cannot effectively respond and control such an infectious disease like COVID-19, which is the deadliest in human history, so cooperation and collaboration with civil society are essential strategies. Yet the nature of the citizenry is multilayered, complex, and self-contradictory, as are the starting point for the infection, the host of transmission, and the treatment platform of the disease. The whole of society is required to cooperate with civil society and the marketplace, and so the construction of a collaborative relation with civil society that shows greater sophistication and responsiveness is needed to reflect the opinions and needs of socially vulnerable people, such as nonregular workers, self-employed, women, children, minorities, disabled people, remote residents, and those who are inexperienced in the information processing technologies, all of whom are forced to bear socioeconomic burdens due to the government's unilateral measures. In times of social crisis, the government alone cannot protect and support the socially vulnerable, and so complementary measures are requested such as the empathy, support and financial resources provided by volunteers from civil society. Cooperation with civil society is imperative to monitor human rights violations, bureaucratic errors, abuses of power, corruption, dysfunction, and financial tricks arising from the government's prevention and control administration, as well as to improve safety, inclusiveness, equality, accountability, transparency, and so forth. As the prevention and control policy is made amid uncertainty and ambiguity, adjusting gradually with partial and on-site modifications and supplements through exchanges and interactions with civil society is inevitable. No matter whether the government succeeds in developing reasonable control measures or not, it is civil society where the implementation is ultimately carried out and the actual services are provided. It is on the sites where the daily lives of citizens are carried on and where they telecommute, purchase remotely, e-learn, and share information in pursuance of the social distancing required for prevention.

However, the prime task in establishing cooperation with civil society is the inevitable delay due to the conversion time taken to go through the government for the citizens' participation. This delay is a crucial obstacle in responding to crises calling for a speedy response, crises so critical as to be a matter of life and death. Yet it is not easy to get citizens to take on the governing process. In a crisis like that caused by COVID-19, serious factors are hesitation over possible violations of the freedom to assemble and associate and psychological resistance to participating and deliberating in the public realm while maintaining social distancing and avoiding face-to-face meetings. Even when participation and deliberation via digital devices are presented as alternatives, the inequalities among socioeconomic underdogs in the ability to participate due to inefficiencies in participation or asymmetries of information processing capability remain obstacles. Needless to say, participation without deliberation threatens the fundamental nature of collaborative governance. There is no reason to believe that a member of civil society would not fall into the trap of "disaster egotism", such as trying to prioritize collective interests, distort civil preferences or take a free ride through the separation of authority and responsibility. It is then that the demand for establishing social norms in civil society becomes critical because, otherwise, a "social crisis" arises.

Summing up, human civilization has come to face a "total crisis". In fact, even most Western countries that have long been regarded as in the lead of modern civilization have repeatedly stumbled and have failed to break free from the shackles of COVID-19. Meanwhile, South Korea has shown a leading performance in responding to the pandemic. Needless to say, looking at such a contrast, any social scientists living in this contemporary world might feel obliged to conduct research and delve into the root causes of such a contrast. It may have originated from a priori assumptions of scientism, rationalism, and reasonable discourse as the only alternatives of human civilization, which now could be evaluated as one of the West's or modernity's biases. On the contrary, South Korea's success seems to owe much to warmth, emotionalism, commitment and sacrifice, instead of to self-interests, contracts, self-centeredness, and egoism, ranging far afield from the basic assumptions of mechanical modernity. This is why South Korean familism draws special attention. This may not be a place simply to shed light on the root causes of success in preventing and controlling the disease but rather to indicate a starting point to discuss the opening a new chapter of modern civilization. As we enter the postmodern society, the diagnosis has been rendered that modern civilization, based on scienticism, egoism, individualism, contractualism, and solid mechanism, is on its last legs. There is also a curiosity driving the search for a dialectic alternative for the next phase of civilization. In that respect, the relative weight of the alternative shown by South Korean society is never light. Yes, "total crisis" can be turned into "total opportunity" for all of us depending upon what we will be learning from this pandemic.

June 2021
Seoul, Korea

1 Introduction

Crises produce various shocks and changes in our lives. Recent experiences include the outbreak of COVID-19. Many have already forfeited their lives and work, lost confidence in the existing order, and long for a new form of governance and leadership as well. In fact, the global spread of pandemics has greatly changed governance systems and thus human history.

The Eustian plague, which is speculated to be the SunFest of today, had prevailed throughout the 6th to 8th centuries. It spread throughout Europe and cut the total population in half. This led to the fall of the empire era, in which one emperor exerted strong centralized ruling power in Europe, and the emergence of the medieval feudal system, in which the lords of each province exercised autonomous rights (Jin, 2020.04.08). The Black Death, which swept through Europe in the 14th century, developed into a catastrophe in which a third of Europe's population died, causing a huge labor shortage. This again changed the feudal production system and led to the birth of the bourgeois working class on the basis of the capitalist production system. The Spanish flu, which killed more than 50 million people around the world in the early 20th century, sparked the idea of prioritizing one's own national interests, thwarted the spirit of international cooperation, and triggered nationalism and protectionism among nations, which led to the Great Depression of the 1930s, which, in turn, became the immediate cause of World War II (Lim, 2020.07.06, p. 3).

There is already a heated debate about which governance or leadership style is more valid and efficient in responding to the COVID-19 pandemic. China has led the contentious debate. In a commentary, the *People's Daily* in China took the position that resolute and competent authoritarianism is more efficient and legitimate than a glazed democracy, as if Chinese-style socialism is an ideal alternative (Chun, 2020.06.02). On the other hand, *The Washington Post* (Rogin, 2020.03.11) expressed the view that South Korea's success in combating the pandemic showed that democracy based on openness and transparency is an effective alternative.

DOI: 10.4324/9781003240709-1

However, if South Korea's success owes much to democracy, it becomes difficult to explain why the openness and transparency of democracy in the United States and Europe as well failed to prevent and control the pandemic. As if conscious of this, another explanation was extended that South Korea's success in the prevention of the pandemic owed much to the surveillance state, controlled society and collectivism of East Asia. In short, its success is not due to China's rival model but because it belongs to the Chinese model in a broad sense. As a representative case, Guy Sorman saw that South Korea's success in responding to the pandemic, like China's, owes much to the great influence of Confucianism, trusting intellectuals and experts, complying with orders more easily, and treating individuals after groups (Son, 2020.4.29).

In fact, this is nothing more than a perennial debate. With China emerging as an important variable in international relations, it has been quite some time since the debate began over whether authoritarian meritocracy or liberal democracy was a viable model that would ensure the efficiency of state administration. No matter how efficient the Chinese system is, the criticism has been centered on how the benefits of such a system have simply served as a logical basis for justifying the emergence of a new class based on performance, along with the argument that if an outcome is not shared among individual people, it is of no use. Corruption, which is rampant within and beyond the new class, was also pointed out as an issue. Currently, we are watching further developments in China. However, with the collapse of the era of American unipolarity rooted in the globalization of the world and the rise of China, it has become difficult to dispute that the outcome of this debate will be one of the core foundations for the future of human civilization.

When we succeed in identifying the driving forces of South Korean governance as demonstrated in the process of responding to COVID-19, it does not mean simply that we have become able to specify a more effective means to prevent and control infectious diseases. Even if South Korea is to reveal a normative standard of governance, which has shown relatively high performance in preventing and controlling the COVID-19 pandemic, we also face an additional challenge to figure out whether we are able to transplant such a model of governance to other countries. This is because doing so will enable us to determine whether South Korea's governance model could be the norm for the future governance of the world. In that respect, more sincere and comprehensive research is required. However, most of the previous discussions in the literature do not exceed the bounds of a state-centered approach. In addition, classifying South Korea, which unlike China has never employed a city blockade or border closure, in a category like China means nothing more than to repeat the "Asian values" debate. That is, just as the patriarchal and authoritarian tradition of Confucian culture has been evaluated as the engine of the rapid economic development of East Asian countries, the success factor of K-prevention during the epidemic also owes much to the root causes of Asian values.

However, the concept of Asian values has been criticized from many different perspectives, and it requires more than simple and superficial approaches, like Asian values, to explain South Korea's success. At the heart of the counterarguments against Asian values, there is a question of whether the legacy of Confucianism suggests only a patriarchal structure of society. Some have already pointed out that it was only a framework mobilized to justify Asia's unique system of authoritarian development. However, contrary to the obedience culture of Confucianism, South Korea held general elections amid the outbreak of COVID-19, and there were also antigovernment demonstrations and street protests that called for improvements of working conditions. The nation's modern political history has been stained with political strife and resistance, such as opposing authoritarian rule. There is also the question whether South Korea, as one of the leading information societies, still stays under the same level of patriarchal structure as in the past. Whereas the success of K-prevention and control of the epidemic owe much to the heritage of Confucianism, one of the questions that must be answered is why South Korea has shown different modes of response in fighting against COVID-19 than China, which is the birthplace of Confucianism.

With such questions to be answered, it is necessary to identify the key factors that have contributed to the successful implementation of South Korea's COVID-19 prevention and control policy in 2020. To this end, considering that COVID-19 is a transboundary disease and therefore very naturally brings about social crisis, we are compelled to analyze the success factors of crisis response in South Korea through a literature review of crisis governance and cultural heritage of the country.

2 Seeking crisis response implementation governance

1. Spread of COVID-19 and social crisis

COVID-19 is an infectious disease that caused a serious social crisis due to its transboundary nature and rapid proliferation. It quickly interrupted daily lives and created a vicious circle that changed the social context. More than anything else, in international relations, it very easily crossed the borders of nation states, creating a vicious circle between nationism and globalism. In order to block such a circle, border closures or "distancing" between countries are among the alternatives. However, such measures threaten the global economic system in this era of globalization, sparking inward-looking tendencies and isolationism and shrinking economic activities among nations. In this case, it is natural that global governance based on the neoliberal system will be in jeopardy.

This protectionist tendency sparks the reshoring of overseas production facilities to the home country, weakening the energy toward hyperglobalization and expanding the room for exercising relative autonomy of individual countries. At the global level, deepening economic inequality among individual countries hinders the recovery and revitalization of the worldwide economy. When the economy slows down, the consciousness of political sovereignty and the egoism of individual countries striving to recover from such economic difficulties are further reinforced. This again conflicts with globalism, which is aimed at promoting the economic prosperity of the world. Therefore, prioritizing the interests of individual countries based on democratic polity is susceptible to collision with cosmopolitanism, which is aimed at universal benefits throughout the world.

However, in order to respond to environmental pollution and climate change, seen as key factors behind the outbreak of infectious diseases, pan-global solidarity and cooperation are vital. Since the COVID-19 quarantine of a country is linked to that of other countries, immediate and humanistic support for other countries is requested, in addition to mid- and long-term approaches, total health care systems, and, more fundamentally, the issue of using infectious disease–related medical technologies as public intellectual property on a pan-global level. This is not easy to achieve without a whole-of-the-world approach (Kauzya, 2020, p. 3) and cooperation. The guarantee of employment, as the basis for health care and the maintenance of marginal income associated with human fundamental rights or pride, is also difficult to achieve with closed nationism that pursues only the benefits of a single country.

In this process, it becomes usual to account for the efforts of developing and sharing diagnostic kits, medical equipment, and preventive treatment as manifestations of humanity. However, when we take a closer look at the reality of the operations and cooperation, we commonly see that they prioritize the interests of quarantine and/or medical product suppliers under the pretext of humanism. This tells us of the emergence of "disinfection capitalism" or "medical capitalism". Politically, it is not unusual to see that disaster diplomacy undermines the authenticity of international cooperation seeking to prioritize the interests of individual donor nations or the improvement of international relations favoring the donors. However, it is not easy to promote international cooperation while ignoring disinfection capitalism or disaster diplomacy. In international relations, it should be remembered that realistic interests are a key driving force.

Changing context and looking at domestic relations, COVID-19 is also found to repeatedly bring about contradictions and conflicts between individualism and nationism due to its transboundary nature. Originally, the state was regarded as having the responsibility to take care of individual freedom and security. Of course, it also ought to maintain the physical freedom and privacy of individuals. This is particularly a basis of the legitimacy of a state, especially in the case of a democratic polity. However, due to the nature of COVID-19 spreading beyond the boundaries among individuals, groups and realms, a state cannot help but to limit individual freedom for the protection of individuals. In order to prevent the spread of the virus, the state must force the entire community to follow rules such as complete lockdowns of cities, social distancing and the obligation to wear masks when using public transportation.

This also brings in the problem of the "securitization of health" (Rushton, 2011, pp. 779–796). The social environment in which disease transcends social boundaries with ease increases the legitimacy of state centeredness as it does during wartime, and, furthermore, the state cannot resist disciplining its citizens without great hindrances. To ensure the safety of public health, there is a perception that the state's compulsory action is inevitable (van de Pas, 2020, p. 18). In this case, individuals are no longer independent, and it becomes difficult to maintain independent control over one's own dignity or the right to freely dispose of one's own body. It is then not easy to consider or take into account the interests of the socially weak, especially under such uniform measures taken by the state. The monism of state power that takes the entire community as one unit cannot take it into account without disregarding the case-specific characteristics of individuals. However, not only does infection by the disease show a socioeconomically differential distribution by penetrating the socioeconomic vulnerable (M. Kim, 2020, p. 69), but the social, economic, and physical losses and risks suffered by individuals caused by the infection also vary. Nevertheless, the state can only deal with it universally and unitarily, even though there are some variations.

In addition, if we venture to take aggressive measures such as social distancing or blockades of cities or other areas for quarantine purposes, this not only dramatically shrinks the economy but also puts economic costs and burdens on individual people. The psychological contractions and discomforts experienced by the locals are also a problem. If these economic and social costs are disregarded for the sake of efficient quarantine, the public's dissatisfaction with them builds up, and they begin to resist government policy. In the case where they ease up and avoid proactive prevention measures due to such concerns, it aggravates the spread of infectious disease and only further deepens distrust of the government's ability to control them. It is a kind of policy dilemma where neither option can be actively chosen by the government (Kim & Cho, 2020, p. 438).

This leads to doubt about the efficiency and legitimacy of government-led health and sanitation policies, but it does not mean that the government may turn away from a community-wide response that overcomes individualism. This is because the disease, which transcends social boundaries, is a determined threat not only to the individual but also to the entire order of the social community. In this case, a representative government naturally cannot but fall into contradictions in its operational structure. This is, in turn, because the universal benefits of the entire community raise questions about who represents or can represent whose interests in the representation process.

Therefore, the argument that the state's quarantine activities should be applied proportionally according to individual circumstances instead of uniform and unilateral approaches becomes more persuasive. It simply reminds us that the political control and monitoring of the state's quarantine policies by the people are inevitable. However, while political control requires a reflection of individual characteristics and interests, crisis management in health and hygiene is, after all, based on scientism, which is oriented toward universality and generality. The fact is that quarantine activities are ultimately a matter of medical science. Therefore, how to overcome the conflicts between politics and science is another dilemma.

2. Contradictory issues in crisis response strategies

The essence of social crisis arising in the process of responding to COVID-19 is a question of conflicts and mismatches, of whether to follow monism or centralism, like globalism, nationalism, and scientism, or pluralism, or decentralism, such as nationism, individualism, and political requests. As they vary in dimensions and contexts, the conflicts and contradictions between the two are difficult to resolve over time systematically, eurythmically and sequentially. Rather, the possibility of distorting the nature of the problem increases as contradictions are repeatedly reproduced. Therefore, responding at the first step is critical in problem solving. To escape this type of vicious structure, the key challenge is to break away from time constraints and problem ambiguity and uncertainty, which can be regarded as the nature of crisis. A crisis requires a rapid response, and a sophisticated and on-site adhesion approach is required in the diagnosis of symptoms.

Therefore, agile governance (Janssen & van der Voort, 2020; Moon, 2020) or evidence-based governance (Yang, 2020; Lancaster, Rhodes, & Rosengarten, 2020) has a reasonable appeal. Agile governance seeks to ensure speed by enabling the government to respond reactively and preemptively through the centralization of decision-making structures and the development of software. In this respect, it is assumed that a very broad political consensus is already in place for the direction of policy in a broad sense, such as the total use of available resources for quarantine activities. Evidence-based governance, on the other hand, seeks an approach based upon de-ideological, field-oriented, rational measurements and assessments to ensure a preemptive response to a foreseen situation. It is nothing but a decentralized approach in the sense that an on-site and fact-oriented approach is emphasized. It has the propensity of being in tune with the swiftness of agile governance because it is dependent upon the unitary nature of scientism, separate from the process of coordinating diverse and multiple political interests through citizen participation. On the other hand, the rapidness of agile governance has conflicting elements with the prioritization of swiftness in that it will take a relatively long time to come to any conclusion if fact-finding is conducted through a decentralized approach based on various sites. This is believed to be the result of mutual conflicts between centralized and decentralized approaches of the perceived frameworks of governance. However, both are the same in that they are trying to respond to crisis at the decision-making level from the standpoint of the state.

Meanwhile, those who want to explore crisis response at the service delivery level often suggest resilient governance (Brousselle et al., 2020; Giustiniano et al., 2020) and adaptive governance (Djalante, 2012; Țicla'u et al., 2020) strategies. Resilient governance seeks a return to the rule of law and the restoration of routine, on the premise that political consensus on the desired future situation has already been reached. In that respect, it is no different from seeking a speedy recovery of routine from deviations. However, adaptive governance presupposes a kind of evolutionary learning process on the premise of the adaptation process for the gradual overcoming of structural contradictions. It also implies deviance and illegality since it is trying to gradually conform to the practical needs of the people by complying with the situational and impromptu needs (Boin & Lodge, 2016, p. 292). The problem is that such a gradualist approach has its own limitations as an alternative to overcome crisis that must be achieved under time constraints. Resilient governance, on the other hand, implies swiftness because it suggests an impromptu restoration. On this point, both approaches collide with each other. The conflicting elements of adaptive governance are also the same in the relationship with agile governance, even though they are at different levels and in different contexts. Conflicts arise between the slowness of adaptive governance and the swiftness of agile governance.

However, from an epistemological point of view, while resilient governance implies a centralized response for the immediate recovery of everyday life, adaptive governance suggests a decentralized strategy, implying close and gradual adaptations on the spot. After all, agile governance, evidence-based governance, resilient governance, and adaptive governance as crisis response strategies caused by COVID-19 are mutually conflicting, confrontational, and contradictory in that they are based on centralized and decentralized perspectives in their epistemological frameworks of governance.

3. Types of crisis response implementation governance

The key challenge of governance as a crisis response strategy for overcoming COVID-19 is to resolve and ease the vicious structure created between centralization and decentralization in its epistemological framework. However, it seems to be clear that rational decisions relying on systematic and sequential developments at the same level are powerless in solving problems on their own in situations where the problems are different in dimensions and have built-in mutually conflicting and contradictory relationships. Therefore, even if it may be considered a decision that is made in disorder or chaos when it is approached from a unidimensional perspective, it requires an approach that positively evaluates and encompasses multiple dimensions. The garbage can model (GCM) is a typical case. Designed by Cohen, March and Olsen (1972), GCM means that we can come to a conclusion when a stream of problems that people are interested in, a stream of choices that says what led to a decision, a stream of solutions that seeks the ways to fix the problems, and a stream of energy from the participants that speaks to support and encouragement by those involved all interact among themselves and beyond one another's flows. Therefore, GCM is effective in explaining irrational and haphazard decisions. However, of course, it has limitations in examining the linkages between such problems and the methods analytically, logically, and preemptively. Therefore, the significance of GCM as a strategic alternative to solving problems is cut by half, even if it may work as a tool for posthumous explanation.

This problem led Kingdon (2003) to propose the multiple-streams framework (MSF). MSF explains that a policy window opens, an agenda is chosen, or a policy is decided when a coupling is made among interactions of a problem stream associated with the perception of government problems, a policy stream as a process for seeking problem-solving alternatives in the policy community, and a politics stream that develops around agenda selection pressures provoked by elections and elected officials. At this time, these three streams are not completely independent, but each has some degree of independence from the others and is presupposed to have a system with an exogenous nature. This is like the issue of centralization and decentralization, which refers to relative concepts in their basic nature, so that they are independent from one another and at the same time interconnected. As a result, it was seen that the kinds of outcomes made through interactions among the streams were determined by the flow modes and ratio of each of these factors and also by the procedures related to each of them.

MSF is very distinctive in its emphasis on situational variables such as social support and the exercise of influences, taking special heed of political streams or national moods. This means that it is important to take on the context. However, MSF has limitations in assuming that a stream flows through inertia until the window of policy making opens, since it basically recognizes and treats policy takers as passive objects. Above all, its discussion does not extend to policy implementation by focusing primarily on setting agendas or explaining decision making. Of course, no attempt has been made to explain the delivery of services by the government or after the implementation stage, such as feedback. The important thing is that it is necessary to ensure speed by institutionalizing the policy process in order to decide policies under the pressure of situational change, and then the plausibility that it will not be able to reflect situational changes occurring over time would be increased. It falls into a kind of paradox between swiftness and adaptiveness.

Taking this into account, Boswell and Rodrigues (2016) not only expanded the discussion to the implementation stage but also paid special attention to the relationship between political stream and problem stream. As a result, they covered and put the policy implementation forms and the reaction scenarios of government organizations and institutions created by mingling of the two streams into four different groups and verified each group according to the specific policy cases of the United Kingdom. According to them, the two criteria constitute policy implementation scenarios. First, the politics stream is seen as a phenomenon in which organizations or institutions involved in solving social problems place political pressure on the central government for support and coordination in order to secure their legitimacy and necessary resources, and, accordingly, the central government coordinates, manages, and supports the relevant institutions. In other words, the coupling efforts extended by elected officials, policy innovators or policy entrepreneurs linking the problem stream with the alternative stream is the politics stream. Second, the problem stream is to be understood from the perspective of problem fit between problems and problem-solving alternatives. At this time, the problem fit is an outcome of the assessment made according to the degree to which alternatives of the central government to solve social problems are executed in the direction that local government agencies or organizations that intercede with the problem stream expect and pursue. Accordingly, it is seen that when both the politics stream and the problem fit are strong, there is consensual implementation, and in cases where the politics stream is weak and the problem fit is strong, there is bottom-up implementation. If the politics stream is strong and the problem fit is weak, there is coercive implementation by the politics stream in a decoupling relation with the problem stream, and when both the political stream and the problem fit are weak, nonimplementation takes place since there is a very weak linkage among the three streams, or no couplings.

However, this categorization work by Boswell and Rodrigues (2016) basically reveals the limits of a state-centered approach. It contains limits of making light of cooperation with civil society by approaching policy implementation under a framework of government only and not from a governance perspective. In a crisis, civil society and, more specifically, individual citizens cannot just passively wait on developments taking place at the government level. In order to respond to the urgency reflecting the contextual conditions of crisis response, the work of minimizing the conversion costs arising in the process of going through the government needs to be prioritized. It is also awkward to downplay the roles of policy leaders, led by citizens or the media, which are under the pressure of time limits in contemplating various alternatives, trading off political orders and facilitating dialogue. More aggressively, it is possible that civil society might be hesitant in cooperating with government and may want to resolve crises by itself because of little or no trust in the state. More importantly, this categorization overlooks the fact that a whole-of-society approach encompassing all involved is inevitable in the sense that it provides all available resources for efficient crisis response (Kauzya, 2020, p. 3).

More fundamentally, it presupposes a strong government and strict distinction between public and private arenas, connoting a Western cultural bias. Therefore, it is not easy to apply these frameworks generally and universally to non-Western societies going beyond cultural boundaries, where the distinction between the public and private arenas is unclear. More importantly, in a crisis caused by infectious diseases such as COVID-19, it should be remembered that civil society cannot but be considered a key influencer for the prevention and overcoming of infection, as it is the final site of the crisis of infection and the starting point from which the problem of infection begins. In a policy dilemma that creates a vicious circle, such as the COVID-19 response policy, the inherent inconsistencies of the problem make it difficult for the government to develop a flawless rational solution (Zohlnhöfer & Rüb, 2016, p. 4). Since it is one of the characteristics of crisis situations that makes it difficult to develop solutions for problems is their uncertainty and ambiguity, it is inevitable that the shortfalls arising in the process of developing solutions should be left to civil society to supplement through on-site response and adjustments. Bowtell (2020.03.06) argues that civil society's participation in crisis response is an integral part of learning from past infectious disease cases such as HIV.

Therefore, if we deal with the implementation tasks of crisis response policies from a standpoint of the relationship between the state and civil society and not within the framework of a state, we cannot help but to take the state, civil society and crisis situations as the determining factors of governance. It is said that a society's mode of response to crisis situations is to be decided according to the severity of the crisis, the response of the state, and the degree of civil society's response to it. The more severe the crisis and the more positive the government's response to it, the greater the confidence of civil society will be in the government (Kauzya, 2020, p. 4), and the higher the government's credibility, the more active the response of civil society toward the government will also be. Therefore, the level and form of citizen participation may well be decided according to the degree of severity of crisis situations and the degree of positiveness of government response evaluated by civil society, and, accordingly, the form of implementation governance of the crisis response policy will also be decided.

In Table 2.1, type I indicates a case where both the degree of severity of crisis situations and degree of positiveness of government response as perceived by civil society are high. The crisis situations are serious, the government responds to them actively and efficiently, and so civil society's trust in the government is high. Therefore, civil society also wants to collaborate and respond actively to overcome crisis situations. The possibility of listening to each other (Kauzya, 2020, p. 3), collaborating horizontally, and coupling in a balanced manner increases as both the state and civil society

Table 2.1 Types of crisis response policy implementation governance

Degree of positiveness of government response \ Degree of severity of crisis situation	High	Low
High	I. Cooperative (balanced) governance	II. Passive (mobilization) governance
Low	III. Proactive (autonomous) governance	IV. Laissez-faire (defensive) governance

want to actively respond to crisis situations. To borrow the framework from Boswell and Rodrigues (2016), the stream of the state, the stream of civil society, and the stream of problems are in strong cohesion amidst the interactions among them. According to Kooiman's typology seeking a neutral perspective on the state and civil society as well (2010, p. 83), it is equivalent to co-governance. They want to give each other's identities and autonomies the same weight and solve problems together for the common purpose of overcoming crisis situations. This is frequently found in communication governance, public and private arenas partnerships, and network regimes between the state and civil society. Seen from a civil society perspective, it could be defined as cooperative governance or balanced governance.

Type II is a case where the degree of severity of crisis situations as perceived by civil society is low, whereas the degree of positiveness of the government's response is high. Even though the situations are not very serious, the government responds to them actively, and so civil society responds to the crisis situations passively as an outcome of its high trust in the government. Therefore, while the government plays a leading role in responding to crisis situations, civil society simply reacts and engages in a passive governance. Government and civil society settle into a loose coupling relationship, which could be referred to as mobilization governance due to the relatively large initiative power of the government. In Kooiman's typology (2010, p. 83), it is hierarchical governance. When the initiative power of the government is further strengthened as top-down intervention forms a mainstream, it leads to a decoupling relationship between the government and civil society and finally builds a vertically multilayered structure that is government-friendly. This is why there could be a growing risk of falling into populism.

Type III is a case where the degree of severity of crisis situations as perceived by civil society is high and the degree of positiveness of the government's response is low. Despite the seriousness of the situation, there is a low level of trust in the government since the government's response to the situation does not seem appropriate. In this case, civil society is more likely to respond with further active initiatives by leading the crisis response on its own, and this results in the formation of proactive governance. Since the government and civil society form vertical relationships that are civil society–friendly, they organize an autonomous governance led by civil society. In this case, the government and civil society remain in a loosely coupled relationship. According to the typology of Kooiman (2010, p. 83), it is self-governance. It tends to be favored mainly by political liberals and presupposes the self-generating power of civil society.

Type IV is a case where both the degree of severity of crisis situations and the degree of positiveness of the government response that civil society recognizes are low. Since the government's response to crisis situations does not seem to be appropriate, and, in addition to that, the crisis situation itself is not serious, civil society reacts passively. Since both the government and civil society are responding passively, there is a high possibility that either of them falls into distrust with the other and loses aggressiveness in overcoming crisis situations. In such a case, the state and civil society are decoupled, act independently from each other, and become helpless in responding to crisis situations. As the formation of governance itself is avoided or there is reluctance to do so, it results in defensive or laissez-fare governance.

In order to move from passive governance to proactive governance in such a structured framework, strengthening the role of civil society works as the determining factor. This is because civil society should be able to put pressure on the power elites not to maintain an old order any longer, which leads to passive governance or a double-layered structure between the government and civil society.

3 South Korea's sociocultural characteristics and state

1. Low-trust society and flat state

The perception of the state shared among the people of a country is usually shaped by their experience with a variety of factors, including its history and culture, its founding process, its orthodoxy, and its political system. From this perspective, South Korea can be identified as a "flat state". Kang (2007) reported that the state in South Korea has a very wide jurisdiction, like type IV countries in the four-division model that Fukuyama (2004, p. 23) theorized, but the penetration power to enforce or govern the will of the state and make civil society accept it is relatively weak and described as that of a "flat state".[1]

However, Fukuyama (2004, p. 21) tried to identify the scope of the state on the basis of functional boundaries or goals governed by the institutions or organizations of a state. In Western society, where the distinction between public and private sectors is clear, the scope of the state seen from a legal perspective may not differ much from that of the state's actual influence, but in places where the division between public and private sectors is not clear, such as in South Korea, the boundaries of actual influence can be measured when it is seen from the state's informal influence. When the power of the state is grasped on the basis of the relative degree of law enforcement power or power to plan and implement policies (Fukuyama, 2004, p. 22), such an approach would be appropriate in Western society, where they presuppose a dichotomic role division between the state and civil society and a contractual relationship between the two role arenas. However, it might be necessary to review it together with the degree of civil society's capacity to accommodate such state power, where the distinction of boundaries between the two is ambiguous, as in South Korea. In that respect, Fukuyama's indicators are no different from those that include a Western cultural bias. Considering this, it is required to examine the scope and power of the state not on the basis of laws or institutions but on the extent of their real influence produced by the exercise of such power.

DOI: 10.4324/9781003240709-3

Sociocultural characteristics and state 15

First, the state of South Korea has a very wide range of jurisdictions. The reason for this can be found in the epistemological origin of Confucianism, which was passed through the Chosun dynasty.[2] People are perceived in Confucianism as passive objects protected by the emperors and their agents as if they were their parents and teachers. This is very clearly stipulated in the records of the *Taejongsilok*,[3] volume 5 in June of King Taejong year 3. The people are likened to a suckling newborn baby there (Choi, 2008, pp. 163–164). Since then, such a way of projecting and recognizing the state from the framework of familism has become one of the dominant forms of thinking that permeates South Korean society.

However, such a family-centered way of thinking has the effect of blurring the lines between the formal and informal dimensions of government organizations or institutions. As the area of personal intimacy extends to that of public relations through the medium of the family, the boundaries dividing the two become unclear and further expand into a state. This is because we recognize the state from the perspective of "SusinJaega ChikukPyungChunha [修身齊家 治國平天下]",[4] which is a phrase taken from *Great Learning* (大學), one of the four great scriptures of Confucianism. Furthermore, such an ambiguous boundary provides an opportunity for the intervention of the state, which is the real substance of public authority, to spread into whole segments of society, including the home (Park, 2018, p. 414).

In this way, the jurisdictional expansion of the state could also be indebted to the introduction of a repressive system by the colonial rule of Japan, which began after the end of the Chosun dynasty with no social countervailing forces in place. It nominally set out the rule of law, but it had become a common practice to extend the scope of state power beyond the law. Its representative example is administrative guidance,[5] which has become a practice in the governance of South Korea since the Japanese colonial period, as the state indirectly exerts influence in order to carry out its own will, even if it is not under the official jurisdiction of the government.

The end of colonial rule and liberation from it led to a very intense ideological struggle in South Korea. Even to these days, after the end of the Cold War between the West and the East, it has remained the only divided country in the world, where a liberal democratic system and communist socialist system compete for ideological superiority. As a result, it has become very common to judge and define every movement according to the standard of ideology. The influence of state power, in the overreach of ideology, easily crossed the usual boundaries of state power. Various forms of quasi-governmental organizations, effectively led by the government in actual terms, were organized and operated as mobilization tools for ideological struggle.

As the modernization work progressed around government-led economic development, the South Korean model of developmental cooperativism took place (K. Kim, 2018) and expanded the scope of the exercise of state power to markets and civil society. A most favored treatment network was built among senior government officials leading the economic development plan, and the heads of large conglomerates and representatives of organizations in government circles, including unions friendly to the state, brought a virtually unlimited increase in the scope of the exercise of state power along with the routinization of corruption. The military-led authoritarian regimes that emerged in the process exercised virtually unlimited state power, resulting in there being no place where state power could not reach in actual terms.

Since the June Uprising[6] in 1987, South Korea has entered an era of democratization, but the scope of the state's influence remains as large as before. The fundamentalism fighting for moral superiority over one another overwhelmed society amid continuing factional fights between those who had led economic development and those who had fought for democratization in the past. Such faction-to-faction strife brought a division of power elites into progovernment groups and antigovernment groups, even in the NGOs that have been nurtured ever since the advent of the year-87 system (87年 體制).[7] As a result, the scope of the state's influence has been extended to entire social arenas being mediated by the progovernmental NGOs, even up to the point where there should be concern about the rise of populism when it is coupled with the imperial presidential system in South Korea (Jung, 2020, p. 4).

Therefore, it is common for the scope of state influence exercised by the South Korean government to exceed the boundaries of the rule of law. This has created the state's influence across a wide range of areas that cannot be easily found anywhere else in the world. With this, Henderson (1968) saw that the structural characteristics of South Korean society were in the "politics of the vortex" where public authority sucks up everything through informal networks. However, such an extraordinarily expanded range of state power exercised is not accompanied by the commensurate penetration power in society.

First, under the theological framework of Neo-Confucianism, which prevailed during the Chosun dynasty after the end of the Koryo dynasty[8] and in the beginning of the Chosun dynasty, state management was not perceived as an administrative issue but rather as an exercise of moral education or discipline. As a result, the king was treated as a symbol of moral norms rather than as a head of administration, and the bureaucrats placed more importance on the indoctrination of the people than on administration. As a result, rather than being competent administrative officers, civil and military officials were more like teachers of the people. If anyone cultivated their own moral sense, they could become a noble and also a public official, and it was an important role to teach the people about the manners and civility of humankind (Kim, 2020.07.17). Therefore, it was difficult to find public management projects in the Chosun dynasty to enhance public interests such as road construction and civil engineering works. There were no roads wide enough and no large warehouses to distribute and store products (Kim, 2018.12.08). It is no wonder that it is difficult to expect executive power or administrative oversight of national projects in such a philosophy-oriented state or country so centered upon thinking.

During Japanese colonial rule, which emerged at the end of the Chosun dynasty, a modern management system was introduced, and the Japanese governed in an authoritarian style. But in addition to the distance between the central government as an agent of the colonial order and the general public, there were more fundamental cultural, historical, racial, and linguistic differences between the colonial overlords and the oppressed, and as a result, there were fundamental limits in the social reception of the state authority.

The space of liberation, which was met without preparation, was not the outcome of recovering national rights through the Koreans' own efforts but rather was given by others outside of the Korean peninsula. Consequently, they were driven into the reality of not having a state at the time of liberation from Japanese rule (Lee, 2020.05.16, p. 11). After that, two countries were established on the peninsula regardless of their own preferences, and it was unavoidable that the inhabitants of the south and those of the north would become members of different political entities. In the south, the Republic of Korea was launched in accordance with the liberal democratic system advised by the United States, but it was a country "built" with external help rather than one "established" by "us" (Choi, 2020.09.01).

Consequently, this "deficient state", which was built passively depending upon the variables created by surrounding countries, has never been able to satisfy its own legitimacy, has never acted in accordance with international strategies established by itself (H. Lee, 2002, p. 74), and has not been able to protect its own people from extreme social turmoil and lack of necessities. It has relied on economic and military support from the United States for the maintenance and operation of the government since it was not able to meet the self-sufficiency of its state finances and the maintenance of a standing army, which are known to be the essential elements of a modern sovereign state. This extremely "needy state" continued for a considerable span of time until the early 1970s, when a five-year economic development plan was successfully accomplished. Therefore, it is natural that it has been difficult for the "vulnerable state" (Choi, 2017, pp. 72–73), characterized by a lack of legitimacy in its nation building and inability to maintain financial and military self-reliance, to get consent and support from the people.

Above all, the extreme ideological confrontations that dominated South Korean society in those days were virtually a power struggle (H. Lee, 2002, p. 17).

This led socialist groups to be given an extreme antigovernment coloring. In such an environment, ordinary people were forced to remain loyal to their preferred ideas and ideologies (H. Lee, 2020, p. 17). In such an ideological or power struggle–oriented society, it is natural to find it difficult for the opposition to support a state based on a particular ideology.

In particular, the outbreak of the Korean War gave fuel to these ideological struggles. More importantly, distrust of national leaders accumulated throughout the war. Less than a month after the outbreak of the war, the United States military took over the power to control the operation of ground forces. The government that withdrew from Seoul broadcasting its will to withhold to the public blew up the Han River Bridge, a river-crossing means of the people. A national defense forces scandal broke out, because of which soldiers starved to death because of corruption by the military's heads. These incidents symbolically showed the limits of such a government. In addition, the paranoia and hypersensitivity of such a vulnerable state aggravated distrust in the government (Choi, 2017, p. 92).

Postwar South Korea was a "frozen state" (Choi, 2017, p. 99). Those who suffered from the war were tantamount to those of a defeated nation, and it was difficult to find any desire or plan to rebuild the country. Concrete plans and projects for national reconstruction were not presented until after the May 16 military revolution in 1961. From that time on, state-led economic development and modernization projects were promoted. It was after the advent of the military government that a standardized form of government management in a modern meaning was introduced for the first time throughout the entire government structure. Paradoxically, however, the affluence attained by the success of economic development led by the authoritarian military government inflamed people's desire for democracy. The constant questions raised about the legitimacy of power and resistance by the antigovernment struggle forces resulted in the separation of social members into forces within the system and dissident forces against the regime.

The advent of the year-87 system led to the era of democratization, but according to H. Lee (2002, p. 38), psychological decompression sickness symptoms overwhelmed society. Suddenly, when they were released from the pressure of being mentally repressed and became free, people undermined and damaged the freedom of others by wielding their freedom recklessly. As confrontations between the economic development–led forces and antidemocratic struggle forces continued, distrust in the ability of democratic government to manage state affairs spread throughout society.

Therefore, in such a society where distrust in the state has been heightened, it is not easy for the state to efficiently exert penetration power for policy recipients. As of the first half of the 20th century, South Koreans had lived during the Chosun dynasty and then the Japanese colonial rule period, without a substantively functioning state, and have lived without a state in their minds during much of the second half of the 20th century, through liberation from Japanese rule, the founding of an independent country, the Korean War, the promotion of modernization through economic development, and the implementation of democratization efforts after 1987 (H. Lee, 2002, p. 18). In these circumstances, the lack of a sense of ownership and being stricken with a victim mentality as a social illness are natural (H. Lee, 2002, p. 16). In such a society, it is very natural that they have a very low level of trust in the state[9] and among members of society[10] as well. In such a low-trust society, the penetration power of the state will also be vulnerable, of course. South Korea, a country that has never been able to run an empire based on national consensus, has never reached success in self-rule (H. Lee, 2002, p. 55).

2. Familism and dual state

Nevertheless, the foundations of South Korean society are fraternity and solidarity based on familism. The family during the Chosun dynasty, in which the connection among the members of a family was strongest, was influenced by Confucianism, and so it was understood as a social unit consisting of descendants who performed ancestral rites together for the same grandfathers. In particular, in the late Chosun dynasty, as the system of succession by primogeniture centered on rich father–son relationships was strengthened, the clan rules system of Confucianism was routinized, and in accordance with it, the clan family (門中) became influential. This was largely influenced by the weakening of the controlling power of the countryside aristocrats (鄉村士族),[11] as cooperative relations between the state and the ruling system run by the countryside aristocrats were weakened. As the aristocrats, who had lost their connection to the state, faced a crisis of survival, they actively gathered and strengthened the forces of the clan family to defend their vested interests on the basis of family connections and especially paternal blood lines. As a result, as the family established horizontal tension in its relations with the state, it became a major strategic unit of social activities and an absolute standard of recognition and deeds throughout society as well (Kwon, 2013a, p. 172).

In particular, such a phenomenon became routinized mainly in and out of the gentry class (兩班).[12] Internally, people with the same surnames made a society, and the eldest son of a family succeeded headship of the social community and managed the family property. At the end of the Chosun dynasty, the concept of family became mixed with paternal clans, kinship groups or houses that were a clan community (D. Kim, 2020, p. 72). This means that the basic units of social composition during the Chosun dynasty were not individuals or families but clans. Instead of each family being organized by a single husband and a single wife, a family was substantiated by pedigree, which was called one's family, encompassing all the segments differentiated into a few or a dozen family cells from a single couple (Takahashi, 2010, p. 44).

However, with the onset of Japanese colonial rule, all citizens began to legally be called individuals and dealt with as atomic entities under the closed leadership of the family heads. Through the household system, Japanese imperialism attempted to reestablish the kinship order that had been maintained under Korean social customs as an atomized family that culminated in the head of the household. This made the family a social unit, constructing a vertical relationship with the state, and had an insular position not to be invaded by the heads of other households. However, because the status of children and wives in the family cell was dependent upon the head of the household rather than being independent individuals (D. Kim, 2020, pp. 83–84), the patriarchy of Confucianism was still reflected in dealing with individuals as a passively acting identity in the hierarchical and differential community.

However, in the 1950s and 1960s, after liberation from Japanese imperial rule, ideas about the traditional family system began to shift somehow to a consciousness of modern family in or around the cities. In cities in particular, the concept of a couple as a modern family was diffused, gradually departing from the traditional and paternity-centered concept of the clan family. Such a change was evident with younger people, the higher educated and the professional class (Kwon, 2013, p. 211).

After the 1960s, as state-led industrialization and subsequent urbanization progressed, the collapse of clan society was accelerated, and the preference for couple-oriented urban nuclear families became mainstream. Park (1985, p. 6) saw it as the emergence of a "forced nuclear family". The nuclear family, having been promoted against their will, did not usher in the individualism as in the self-generated nuclear families of the West. Therefore, South Korean families in this era were not entirely Western, even if they were not traditional (D. Kim, 2020, p. 97). As a result, the values and norms the family have were a complex mix of traditional and modern. The multiple layers and hybridity, where various values and ideologies were juxtaposed with one another, became a common practice. An ambivalent, hybrid, and overlapping family concept formed that catered to and mixed traditional and modern lifestyles according to the needs of the situation (Kwon, 2013a, p. 173).

After the late 1970s, social innovations toward monogamy took place, leading to the formation of a nuclear family with real meaning. As a result, there are a large number of loosely organized family models today in which immediate family members and couples are interconnected with one another by being based on nuclear families centered on couples. Compared to the past, the individualization of family members is progressing faster than ever (Kwon, 2013a, p. 176). In urban nuclear families, the immediate family ideology centered on the paternal blood line is working, but on the other hand, the couple system has worked, establishing a very unusual family concept.

In the 1990–2000s, when industrialization and democratization were further advanced, the greatest changes were made to the family system. Feminism was emergent, various forms of family bonding were socially expressed, and multicultural families increased. As a result, the denotation of family was expanded, and its connotations have also been diversified. In addition, as the proliferation of social media softened the identity of individuals, the traditional family concept of a closed community was weakened, and individuals became able to diversify their own personal identities. As it progressed to a society where knowledge labor forms the core, the division of labor between men and women disappeared, and in this process, "role sharing" rather than role division between couple members expanded. In addition to the existing complexity, this has resulted in a change of mixed multicultural elements with flexible network structures (Kwon, 2016.06.02).

This has led to a bifocal society where individuals as members of a family and groups called families are both valued highly at the same time. After all, South Korean families today are still in a state where, although the traditional family system is gradually waning but continues and its scope is relatively wide, individuals as members of a nuclear family in the modern sense have formed a multilayered and fused complex structure. In the case of the clan family, it can be confirmed by the dual structure that this does not show the same affinity as in the past, but the eldest son of the eldest son as the successor of primogeniture is still active as the center of relatives, while individuals as independent entities of the clan family form a clan assembly and govern properties and all other sorts of matters concerned.

Seen from a social and structural perspective, traditional familism, which aimed for survival and material stability while emphasizing closed and strong cohesion, is gradually losing its past appeal but has not disappeared yet, and it means that the freedom, rights, and self-actualization that one's own self pursues as an individual have become more important. This also changes the relationship among family members to a freer and more horizontal one. Therefore, the scope of blood relatives is changing flexibly as the social environment changes, but the traditional sense of familism that has worked as a basis for survival and living is still working and is one of the key drivers pulling South Korean society together (Kwon, 2016.06.02).

However, the meaning of familism in the traditional sense can be roughly classified into emotional familism and exclusive familism. More than anything else, emotional familism confirms that a family is a home for emotional solidarity and sensible return rather than an axis of interest. When it comes to family members, they willingly endure unconditional and infinite affection, devotion, and sacrifice and do not mind extending such favored treatment. The source of such a consciousness could be said to be an instinctive narcissism that comes from the compassion that an individual shows to other members of his or her family and from equating oneself to one's own family, and more than that. This is the source of the educational zeal of parents dedicated to their children in today's South Korean society and has been a force for the superhuman efforts to drive the rapid industrialization and modernization of society. Despite the fact that individualization, industrialization progress, and social and physical conditions have greatly changed, this emotional familism has taken root as one of the strongest sources of driving power in South Korean society.

However, those who view it from an instrumental perspective (Park, 2004, pp. 102–103) have described it as a manifestation of egoistic familism.[13] One of the reasons why in-group bias, such as devotion to or prioritization of family, goes beyond the benefits of community, general conventional wisdom or the common sense of a society is that it comes from regarding family as a means of social security in later years or as a device to preserve one's property. The idea is that devotion to family is, after all, for oneself. It is like being embarrassed by the revelation of one's family's faults. The reason why South Korean society emphasizes saving face or keeping a sense of shame seems to have originated from such egotism. The flaws within the family's fence are all to be covered, protected, and guarded because it is also a kind of means to protect oneself. It is also why, going beyond common practice, we want to "inherit" the private schools, the media, the corporations, and even the churches, and the hereditary handing over of state power for three generations in North Korea could also be interpreted as no different from what has taken place in the South so far.

On the other hand, exclusive familism is a phenomenon that does not hesitate to treat any people other than family members in the most discriminatory and unfavorable ways. This is interpreted as being no different from the out-group phenomenon of egoistic familism. People have doubts about social members other than their family members, distrust them, and even venture to sever relations. It is a social heritage that was sparked by competition and tension among clan families in the latter days of the Chosun dynasty (Kwon, 2013a, p. 172). This naturally raises the question of whether the relationship between the state and family is seen as disconnected or linked. The disconnection perspective is a binary way of looking at relationships with other families, groups, and even social communities outside of one's own family. Naturally, it is more likely to provoke tension, confrontation, and conflicts. The tensions among clan families or Confucian scholar groups in the late Chosun dynasty, the ideological confrontation between liberals and communists after the liberation period, the conflict between those who insist on economic growth first and the forces struggling for democratization under authoritarian military regimes, and the debates between conservatives and progressives after democratization in 1987 that continue to this day are all largely indebted to the exclusive and outward-oriented familism or disconnection perspective that has dominated South Korean society since the Chosun dynasty. In other words, conflicts and confrontations erupt not because of inevitable clashes over meanings and substances but because of the exclusive and discriminatory sentiments that are preemptively aimed at the other party from the beginning. It is also understood as a form of egoistic familism in that it attempts to strengthen emotional familism by mobilizing exclusive feelings toward the outside. It is simply to denote that the outward-oriented vetocracy is internalized. As a result, conflicts and confrontations have long been embodied in South Korean society. It is why the social conflict index of South Korea is the world's highest (Choi, 2017, p. 641).

The linkage perspective, on the other hand, finds the state as the natural extension of the family. According to the general theory of sociology, when centralized bureaucratic organizations develop, it is very natural that relatives or kin groups are left out or disappear. As the social division of work and the stratification of status progress, kin groups are reduced to the families or organizations necessary for raising children, and the separation of private and public domains deepens. However, in the case of South Korea, not only are state and kin groups or public and private domains not strictly separated, but also the boundaries have continuously been floated. This is because a sense of kindred equating ancestry and offspring is projected onto a larger political and social community outside of kinship by extending the bonds among pure kindreds (Kim, 2020.07.09).

This is a very different phenomenon from that of Western society. In the West, it is generally assumed that the family belongs to the private domain, while politics is considered the public domain. However, Neo-Confucianism regarded the family as a foundation for breeding subjects who conformed to the orders of the state, and it therefore counted as if belonging to a semipublic realm (Kwon, 2013a, p. 160). The sentiments that condone the initiatives of bureaucrats in running states and the institutionalization of dictatorships, the attitude of dual values that prevents public discussions about the pursuit of personal interests, and the attitude of sacrificing one's personal interests for the public good shown by conscientious intellectuals in the course of the democratization movement are interpreted as the outcomes of approaching the state and family from the perspective of linkage

(S. Lee, 2002, pp. 62–63). Therefore, the perception that the basic building unit of society is the family and that the conceptual expansion of the family is the nation and social community as well are understood as a result of understanding the home as a place to discipline for the sake of courtesy and virtue. Lee Yee said in the first heading of the chapter on governance (爲政編) in the *Sunghakjipyo* (聖學輯要),[14] which is a textbook for monarchs, that "the state is inferred from a family". According to the chapter *Taeser* (泰誓),[15] it is said that "only heaven and earth are the parents of all, and only man is the lord of all creation; the truly bright becomes kings, and the king becomes the parents of the people" (Choi, 2008, p. 156).

Maruyama (1995) recognized that as society is perceived from the perspective of Neo-Confucianism, the public is located at the extension of the private, and therefore the distinction between them in Korean society is not clear. Furthermore, that is why the public domain, seen from a vertical axis, is dominated by the private domain. And not only is it not possible to substantially distinguish the private domain, where one deals with oneself and one's own household chores, from the public domain as a political space, where people run the country and the world as well, but also the optimism that once one does well with one's own family chores, one can also do political and public work well. This has created a so-called family state framework that looks at the state and the world from a familism standpoint.

As a manifestation of family morals governing these family relationships, people perform ancestral rites, practice filial piety and maintain good brotherhood. However, this family morality is perceived not simply as a norm governing private relationships but also as an absolute and public norm for maintaining social order outside the family. It is also understood that contributing to the state and making a name for history are counted as the greatest filial services to the parents (Choi, 1997, pp. 189–190). It means that they equate family with country. Such a strengthening of family-centeredness and the emergence of a family state are linked to the concept of public and private domains in Neo-Confucianism that emphasizes concentric cooperation among family members (Choi, 2006, p. 1).

Therefore, in South Korean society, a "family state" based on emotional familism, egoistic familism and exclusive familism has become a key framework for understanding social community. However, since the 1990s, the Western concept of individualism has been strengthened in traditional familism, and today, with the addition of the modern concepts of the "contract state", "family state", and "contract state", is forming a double layer. In Western society, South Koreans saw the paradox of crude egoism as self-destructive and self-defeating and counted the spirit of contracting and complying with others to solve the problem of selfishness as a civic virtue (Hwang et al., 1996, p. 29). Westerners wanted to solve the problem of selfishness through an external device called system and contract (Choi, 2008, p. 172). And it is the administrative state in the modern meaning to implement such contractual relations, from which Westerners assume efficiency can be secured. Therefore, in the South Korean consciousness, a "dual state" is entrenched, where the family state and contract state form a dual layer.

3. Wartime culture and switching state

South Korea has constantly suffered from foreign invasions, and it is not overly exaggerating to say that the nation's history is that of wars. Not merely once or twice did the ravages of war put the country at stake and destroy the lives of the people. As a result of the wars provoked by surrounding powers, where continental and maritime forces fought for the control of the Korean peninsula, the country was frequently ruined or its ruling power was replaced. Recently, the damage due to colonialization caused by Japanese aggression and the Korean War between the North and South instigated by the ideological confrontation of the world were truly disastrous. Through these national challenges, South Korean society has repeatedly been trained in social and cultural discipline to respond for sake of its survival. For South Koreans, crisis is no longer an exceptional phenomenon but rather an extension of daily life (Lim, 2020.12.11).

When we recall the ability to respond to crises immersed in the cultural code of South Koreans' wartime culture, the lessons learned from the daily lives of such a culture and compressed into Korean phrases can be found in the most representative idiomatic expressions "hurry up, hurry up [*ppali ppali*]" and "roughly, roughly [*daegang daegang*]". War is characterized everywhere by the collapse of daily lives and the ambiguity of the current situation and uncertainty about the unfolding future. Therefore, people are under pressure to respond quickly so that they can survive. In wartime, which is full of uncertainty, it is not possible to quickly calculate meticulously and respond on the basis of concrete and factual evidence. By responding with agility, we are obliged to adapt to changing circumstances, and therefore we must inevitably take the risk of avoiding evidence-based approaches. We have embodied such wisdom in our daily lives.

War also influenced traditional familism. The exclusive closure and inward cohesion of traditional familism have worked as catalysts accelerating cohesion and compliance in response to external invasions or crises therein. In particular, the constant aggressions and intimidations by surrounding powers have become drivers for the development of these characteristics of familism into a profound social culture. Not only was emotional familism reinforced through wartime turbulence, but in order to deal with social crises such as war, people had no choice but to strengthen their own in-group-oriented emotional familism. Just as protecting one's family in the midst of a war requires infinite love and devotion to family members, it was inevitable to upgrade cohesion and commitment among family members to the next level to overcome such a crisis. Such a tendency has been further reinforced as wars kept on coming and distrust built up that the state would never protect one and one's family. People were driven to believe that all they could trust was the family. In this case, devotion and sacrifice to the family have a dual character in the sense that they are both a foundation and a tool for strengthening emotional familism. The same is true for exclusive familism. Through repeated crises, people were driven to conclude again and again that social relationships outside of the family were not reliable and must be subjected to vigilance and distrust. Of course, such an exclusive familism has caused South Korean society in times of crisis to suffer higher levels of anxiety and hostility among themselves.

However, since the family is also a "family state" according to the traditional concept of familism, emotional familism and exclusive familism have also operated at the state level. Emotional familism and the linkage perspective of the family state were embodied in the stronger sacrifices and spirit of patriotism to the nation during the national crises. This is also a mode of crisis response that is internalized by Koreans. In China during the Japanese invasion, the Nanjing Massacre took place, and the Chinese did not offer any active resistance in defiance of this. In Korea, however, after the March 1 National Independence Movement (三一運動),[16] along with the Blood Squad Group Movement (義烈團),[17] Koreans repeatedly launched a series of heroic deeds by assassinating key figures of the Japanese government and willingly sacrificed their lives. Owing much to emotional familism and exclusive familism, they repeatedly made sacrifices and offered resistance that went beyond common sense. This has been confirmed in many cases where people willingly sacrificed and committed themselves, exceeding their own personal interests in every crisis of the nation. The representative cases are the National Debt Redemption Movement in 1902, which was initiated by the people to voluntarily pay back the government's debts when Korea was on the brink of being absorbed by Japanese imperialism owing to national debts; the gold collection campaign during the 1997 foreign exchange crisis in which people across the nation voluntarily donated gold to the government; and the volunteer activities to clean up containments caused by oil spills on Taean Bando with millions of workdays throughout 2007 and 2008. The unprecedented pace of industrialization and democratization was also possible thanks to a view of the nation that prioritizes the identity of the nation and groups at the expense of individual interests (Sung, 2020.05.16, p. 1). This is no different from talking about the advent of a "self-governing state", in which the people themselves go through a crisis without simply relying on the state in each national crisis. It also connotes a transition to an "auto-administrative state" in the sense that the people play the role the state must play on their own behalf. From the viewpoint of exclusive familism, it can be said that there is a great sense of animosity and resistance to the enemy. Such resistance and sense of animosity to these external enemies became the driving forces that kept the country united in the midst of frequent invasions from the outside and national crises.

In South Korea, the "family state" based on traditional familism and the "contract state" based on modern family relations are coupled with each other. However, when any impact such as war comes from the outside, people have responded to changes in the environment faced by the state by becoming loosely coupled or decoupled. Therefore, South Korea can be summed up as a "switching state" when we see the phenomenon from the viewpoint of the state as an extension of family relations in which the traditional family concept and the modern family concept or traditional familism and modern individualism change their lead positions with each other.

Notes

1 It seems to correspond to the concept of the "awl state" by which Western European countries are labeled due to their governments' high penetration power. Unlike Kang (2007), Park and Kim (2020) have rated South Korea as weak in both the scope and penetration power of the state, suggesting that it corresponds to Fukuyama's type III of the four-division model.
2 This is the last dynasty and ruled the Korean peninsula for 518 years from 1391 to 1897, using Confucianism as a governing ideology.
3 This is a history book about state affairs during the term of the third king of the Chosun dynasty Taejong (1401–1418), written in chronological order.
4 It means "to govern a country and bring peace to all, one should first be able to govern one's family; to govern one's family successfully, one should first learn to govern oneself".
5 "Administrative guidance" is an action in which an administrative agency gives guidance, recommendations and advice for a specific person in order to realize certain administrative purposes in the scope of its own affairs (Article 2, 3 of the Administrative Procedure Act). Under the Act, it is a nonpowered factual act that presupposes arbitrary cooperation by the subject of the guidance.
6 This was an antigovernment protest held nationwide in South Korea June 10–29, 1987. The result was a constitutional amendment for the direct election of the president by the people. It had a significant impact on the democratization of South Korea and the rise of social movements.
7 The year-87 system, which was formed in 1987 through a series of political struggles to democratize the country and efforts for democratic reform, refers to the complex characteristics of the democratized system that emerged through such democratization efforts in South Korea.
8 This was a despotic monarchy that ruled most of the Korean peninsula for about 474 years from 918 to 1392 under the ideology of Buddhism.

28 *Sociocultural characteristics and state*

9 A survey about people's trust in their own government conducted by the OECD found that South Korea was in the lowest group among the 35 member states with 27% in 2011, 34% in 2015, 24% in 2017 and 39% in 2019 (Kwon, 2019.11.14; Park & Ju, 2020, p. 2).
10 Trust among the members of South Korean society is only slightly above 50%, as it was 57.4% in 2016, 56.4% in 2017, 57.1% in 2018 and 55.7% in 2019 (Kye & Hwang, 2020, p. 2).
11 It means a group of blood relatives living in the countryside who could become bureaucrats belonging to the ruling class of the Chosun dynasty.
12 This is a social class unique to the Chosun dynasty that included officials who could participate in politics, families with potential qualifications to become bureaucrats, and even a class of scholars. Originally it had meant bureaucrats including both civilian and military officers but changed to imply a social class in the late period of the dynasty.
13 Park (2004, p. 103) saw family egotism as a belief that "tolerates immoral and unfair in-house bias in order to protect the inclination of giving priority to family". We would like to express this as egoistic familism here with an intention to place it in parallel with emotional familism.
14 This is a political philosophy book written in 1575 by Lee Yee, a famous Confucian scholar of the Chosun dynasty, to teach kings how to govern.
15 One of the chapters in the volume called *Jooser* (周書) of the *Serkyung* (書經), which is a compilation of records written by officers and taught in various countries during the Han dynasty in old China by Confucius and treated as a precious scripture as the social position of the Confucianism rose later on.
16 The 3.1 National Independence Movement was a protest staged by Koreans across the country against Japanese colonial rule, declaring the annulment of the Japan–Korea merger treaty and calling for the independence of Korea on March 1, 1919.
17 The Blood Squad Group Movement was organized in Jilin Province, Manju, China in November 1919 by Kim Won-bong after being greatly impressed by the Koreans who staged independence protests against Japanese imperialism along the lines of the March 1 National Independence Movement. It was a secret organization to achieve the independence of the Korean peninsula from Japanese occupation mainly by deploying the strategies of assassination and destruction. It sparked the spirit of independence movements among Koreans at home and abroad.

4 South Korea's COVID-19 response implementation governance

1. Overview of South Korea's COVID-19 response

There were several phases in South Korea regarding COVID-19, based on the results of a COVID-19 awareness survey conducted 20 times every two weeks from the second week of February to November 25, 2020, by the Korean Research Institute and the status of daily COVID-19 occurrences by each country compiled by Johns Hopkins University in the United States. Reviewing all, there were a relative lull after January 19, a rapidly decreasing trend after a high of 851 cases on March 3 after the start of a surge from the end of February, an increase to 441 cases on August 28, and then a decrease again and finally a surge to 1,237 cases on December 24, 2020.

Similar fluctuations were shown in the degree of severity of the crisis situations[1] and the degree of positiveness of the government response[2] investigated by the Korean Research Institute. By March 3, the degree of severity of the situation rose to 91%, and by August 28 it again showed a degree of severity of 90% (Lee, 2020.11.25, p. 7). On the other hand, a government response assessment showed a low degree of positiveness of 42% around March 3 and 68% around August 28, with the exception of 67% in mid-September (Lee, 2020.11.25, p. 6).

Therefore, based on these two highs, progress can be divided into three parts for convenience: the Former is up to March 3 after the first confirmed case was discovered in January 2020; the Middle is from March 3 to August 28, and the Latter runs to the end of the year after August 29.

If we look at these changes in more detail, it can be seen that the degree of the severity of crisis situations and the degree of positiveness of government response intersect each other five times. The first intersection is seen between the time frames February 11–13 and February 28–March 2 in the Former period, the second between March 27–30 and April 10–13, the third between July 3–6 and July 17–20 (in this case, the outcomes of severity assessment and positivity evaluation are close with a 1% difference), the fourth between

DOI: 10.4324/9781003240709-4

30 COVID-19 response implementation governance

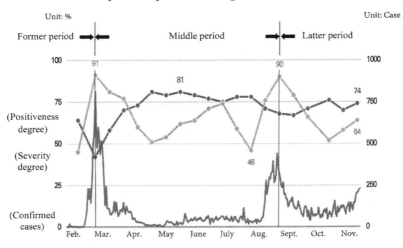

Figure 4.1 Degree of severity of crisis situation, degree of positiveness of government response, and number of new confirmers per day

Source: Compiled from the Korean Research Institute (2020.11.25) and data information from the COVID-19 Data Repository operated by the Center for Systems Science & Engineering (CSSE) at Johns Hopkins University (JHU) in the United States (2020.12.30).

July 31–August 3 and August 14–17 in the Middle period, and the fifth between September 11–14 and September 25–28 in the Latter period.

It reminds us that the various forms of governance were formed all throughout the year. Of course, as we see from the assertion that it is not only impossible but also undesirable to quantify or mathematically verify the MSF (multiple-streams framework) and its working mechanisms (Zohlnhöfer & Rüb, 2016, p. 7), it is arguable whether it is plausible or desirable to categorize governance formation on the basis of mathematical indicators. But it does not mean that quantifying indicators do not tell anything. Sophisticated verification may not be possible, but at least we can estimate the general tendency of change. Since all the intersections are made with more than 50% severity and positiveness as well, it is interpreted here that an active response between the state and civil society was formed around these points and, furthermore, that cooperative governance was made.

Between March 3 and 27, which goes from the Former period to the Middle period, and from August 18 to September 10, which goes from the Middle period to the Latter period, the degree of severity of the situation overwhelmed the degree of positiveness of the response. Therefore, during this period, as civil society responded more aggressively, it could be interpreted that civil society–oriented autonomous governance or proactive governance was formed between the state and civil society.

However, it is observed that passive governance was established three times: the first time from the beginning to February 10 in the Former period, the second from April 13 to 17 in the Middle period, and the third after September 29 in the Latter period. During these time periods, the degree of severity of the situation was lower than the degree of positiveness of the response. Since there was no occasion when the degree of severity of the situation and the degree of positiveness of the response went below 50%, there was no period during which laissez-faire governance worked.

Taken all together, this shows that during the relatively short span of the Former period, passive governance, cooperative governance, and proactive governance emerged interchangeably, and during the Middle period of the year, they were consecutively replaced by proactive governance, cooperative governance, passive governance, cooperative governance, passive governance, and proactive governance. During the latter period, proactive governance, cooperative governance, and passive governance emerged in order. Therefore, it can be noted that the content of crisis response implementation governance changed frequently. Based on the duration, passive governance was up to 206 days, proactive governance was up to 49 days, and cooperative governance depends on how wide you view the scope of the balance, but you can estimate at least 56 days, assuming that the degree of severity of the situation and the degree of positiveness of the response are all within the range of 5% variance from the balanced situation. Of the five cooperative governance occasions, the second, third, and fourth show a change of less than 5% throughout the survey period, so the number of days belonging to these time periods are added, and in the cases of the first and fifth, they are calculated most passively since they go outside the 5% range, so each occasion is estimated as just one day.

Therefore, it is known that during 2020, these three types of implementation governance were frequently replaced by one another, being aligned in the order of passive governance, cooperative governance, and proactive governance according to their duration. It is also valuable to note that passive governance formed a majority. However, seen from the level of civil society, it can be interpreted that the interactions between the family state framework and the contract state framework have been materialized in various forms of governance being pushed by certain opportunities.

2. Manifestation of crisis consciousness and family state frame

Unlike other infectious diseases, COVID-19 causes asymptomatic infections and has significantly different rates of death over generations, so fear about the disease itself is very high. In addition, global fear about the pandemic seems to be higher than that at the outbreak of World War II, as no cure has yet been developed. However, after the outbreak in Wuhan, China, in December 2019, not much concrete and scientific information about COVID-19 was released in South Korea until the first patient was spotted on January 19, 2020. This is why people's fear about the unknown new infectious disease was only exacerbated.

In addition, people's memory about the South Korean government's response to the spread of the MERS infection in March 2015 amplified their anxiety over facing the spread of another infectious disease. At the time, the government's response was not prompt or appropriate. Fourteen days after the first case was confirmed, a public–private cooperative emergency inspection meeting was held for the first time, and the Ministry of Health and Welfare advised the public to avoid close contact with camels and not to consume nonsterile camel milk or meat in a country where camels can only be seen in zoos. More serious was the government's control mechanism. The Korea Disease Control and Prevention Center (KCDC) was reluctant to publicly share information about the infection route and areas. Civil unrest and fear grew, and groundless rumors and fake news were spread as people voluntarily began to share information via social media. This situation was not well managed either. As a result, the world's second-largest number of people were infected and died (Choi et al., 2020, p. 200). This is why people have great distrust in the government.

Once again, the government's initial response was not appropriate. Even though people demanded a border blockade, unlike Taiwan and New Zealand, South Korea did not seal off entry from China, and the initial response was also not swift. The government even advised that people did not need to wear masks. As the spread continued in Daegu City in Gyeongbuk Province, the president also even suggested an easing of response policies. Naturally, concerns about the government's ability to control the spread and distrust of the government were linked to social nervousness. Maintaining government transparency in relations with the people, such as announcing the current state of infections, without offering any clear and consistent countermeasures, served to cause distrust and confusion by evoking fear among the people. In addition, it should be remembered that trust in the state as a flat state in South Korean society has remained consistently low (Chun, 2020.06.12).

It is self-evident that people's consciousness of crisis, such as war, would have been triggered as the fear of disease and distrust in the state overlapped. This is the reason why the switching state phenomenon takes place by changing rapidly from a coupled relationship between the contract state, which is a flat state that usually enjoys a low degree of trust, and the family state into loosely coupled or decoupled relationship between them as the external shock caused by the spread of COVID-19 is given. This also means that proactive governance has become more sweeping. Accordingly, it is confirmed throughout the society that civil society is not simply dependent on the state or simply waiting for the flow but comes to the forefront of responding to the pandemic more actively.

At the medical service level, the public voluntarily came up with innovative ideas for drive-throughs, walk-throughs, and the separation of medical institutions from residential treatment centers, and they went into actual operation. They quickly cooperated with the government for on-site responses, including sharing the information from credit card companies and banks needed to trace infected people, releasing privately owned CCTV and dashcam records, and giving coronavirus relief funds. In nonpharmaceutical terms, the citizens actively collaborated in observing personal hygiene rules such as social distancing, mask wearing and hand washing, and in Daegu, citizens voluntarily isolated themselves from social interactions either by keeping social distance or by refraining from going out even before being recommended to do so by the government (Lim, 2020.07.06, p. 7). In response to the central government's request to produce and supply medical masks, small and medium-sized manufacturing companies voluntarily expanded their facilities, and medical staff rushed to volunteer at no cost in response to an appeal since doctors and nurses were in short supply during the primary stage of the epidemic in the heart of Daegu City and Gyeongbuk Province. There were even doctors who briefly closed their own private hospitals and participated. A guesthouse operator in Daegu City was also impressed and offered free accommodation for the medical staff.

The government sought a 4-T policy, which stands for test, trace, treatment, and trust (Park, 2020, pp. 37–38), whose effectiveness is difficult without active responses from citizens. In Western European countries and the United States, people opposed identity card tracking, the invasion of personal privacy, warrantless movement tracking, and personal data collection, but South Koreans were very receptive. From a family state perspective, there was no reason to hesitate in limiting one's own freedom for the safety and health of society, which is thought of as an extended family. As for the use of masks, it is not an exaggeration to say that citizens themselves led the way. In the early stages of the crisis, because of distrust in the government, they actively volunteered to wear masks in the belief that they could keep their health by themselves despite the government's passive response. And later, as the crisis situation became commonplace, they began to see it as natural to wear masks in order to save face and have a sense of honor. Above all, wearing a mask was encouraged by the feeling of danger that if a mask was not used, the family could be exposed to infection. This is nothing but a manifestation of emotional familism, characterized by inward-oriented devotion and consideration. Social distancing is also the same. Rather than protecting their own health, they actively distanced out of the motivation to keep the health of their families by not spreading disease throughout the community (Lim, 2020.07.06, p. 8).

When wearing a mask was set as an important tool to prevent and control the infectious disease, the government introduced a public mask sales system. However, information about the sales and inventory status of the masks, as well as the locations of pharmacies where citizens were supposed to buy them, was not shared, which was inconvenient for citizens. They developed their own mask application to provide the information and operated their own information sharing networks. To this end, six government departments, public institutions, social clubs, private developers, companies, pharmacists on the front lines, and other civilians and governments collaborated for coproduction. It was citizen-led cooperative governance, through which they created an environment where information was collected and processed, and ordinary citizens developed apps.

Migrant human rights groups, such as With Migrants, translated the government's infectious disease prevention and control guidelines into other languages by their own initiative and shared them on their home pages and through the migrant communities. They also researched the extent of damages suffered by the migrants and called on the government to provide COVID-19 virus relief funds without any discrimination against the migrants. The National Coalition for Prevention of Discrimination Against the Disabled collected emergency relief goods and supported the lives of the disabled who were self-isolated during the period of the virus case explosion in Daegu City and Gyeungbuk Province. They provided care services for inpatients and developed and shared response manuals and living rules. As concerns about the metropolitan epidemic grew, dozens of organizations that had staged human rights campaigns for the LGBTQIA, intermediated by LGBTQIA groups centered around a club in Itaewon, voluntarily organized the LGBTQIA Urgent Countermeasures Headquarters, communicated with the disease control authorities, encouraged health checkups, and conducted human rights abuse counseling (M. Kim, 2020, pp. 70–71).

The basic environmental nature of South Korean society also contributed as a positive factor to the manifestation of voluntary efforts based on emotional empathy. In South Korea, military service is mandatory due to the confrontation between the North and the South. As a result, most male citizens are trained in military service and civil defense programs and learn to share the spirit of sacrifice for the group, comradeship, crisis response routines, and values. The nation's high education level, which boasts a 98% literacy rate, is also one of the reasons people are encouraged to respond rationally and proactively. Since it is not unusual to be exposed to mask wearing due to yellow dust from China, it was not unfamiliar and difficult to be accustomed to the mask wearing required due to COVID-19. Even though people used social media and apps to track infected people and share related information, it was not unfamiliar to the public at all, since this social communication mechanism is already practiced in their daily lives for public purposes such as emergency disasters and traffic jams. South Korea is one of the most advanced countries in the world in the use of information and communication devices in everyday life. It is also one of the additional positive factors that it is relatively easy to procure excellent-quality equipment related to preventing infectious diseases such as masks, diagnostic kits, thermal imagers, anti-bio films, face shields, etc. because they are produced directly in South Korea. In particular, since they developed the diagnostic kits quickly, it greatly contributed at the early stage of infectious disease prevention and control efforts. It was an outcome of the preemptive development efforts initiated by private enterprises before the government requested them to do so.

However, the spread of an infectious disease such as COVID-19 has the nature of enhancing affection for and commitment to the social community in abstract terms, which is driven by emotional familism, and, more concretely, strengthening vigilance and risk consciousness towards neighbors. This is because it is necessary to cooperate with the entire social community to escape from the disease, but people participating in the cooperation itself act as the hosts of infections. Infectious diseases could be regarded as also having the propensity of extending emotional familism and exclusive familism by themselves. Trust in kin groups means that exclusive familism is activated, which pushes distrust in strangers or neighbors other than kin group members and meanwhile promotes emotional familism. This is confirmed by the outcome of regular research by the Korean Research Institute that the reliability of South Korean people increased by 21%, while confidence in strangers decreased by 36% due to COVID-19 (Chun, 2020.06.02).

This gap between emotional familism and exclusive familism was typically seen in mask wearing. Until now, South Korea has shown a high participation rate in mask wearing of 95%. This is partly due to emotional familism and family state consciousness to protect one's own family from disease but also because people like to send a symbolic signal to others that they are participating in the important fight of protecting the whole community from disease infection (Chun, 2020.12.22). This stems from distrusting the outside world other than one's own family. Just as one treats nonfamily members differently, they will continue to treat others differently, so people engage in mask wearing more to avoid giving anyone reason to condemn and reprimand them when their intention is simply to defend themselves. Wearing masks depends a lot on social pressures to save face. On the other hand, a regular survey by the Korean Research Institute showed that 89% supported the government punishing people who do not wear masks (Chun, 2020.12.22). This is not to encourage everyone to join in wearing masks but to indicate that anyone not cooperating in mask wearing does not belong to one's family, since there is no doubt that everyone in one's family wears a mask. Therefore, it is natural that they would like to hold anyone outside the family accountable since they are doing nothing to be held liable for. The belief that no one really backs off and deals with others outside one's family with the most differential treatment is nothing but the manifestation of exclusive familism.

The tendency to hold someone outside one's own family accountable or to free-ride by shouldering the burden of the costs in preventing and controlling disease is also found in social distancing, which is done to protect one's own health and that of the family and is enacted by burdening many segments of society. It puts financial pressure on small business owners, violates the religious freedom of believers who want to participate in worship, and conflicts with the freedom of assembly as seen from the position of demonstrators who want to make political statements. However, the spirit of "I do hope it is not me!" or that of "No one pushes me around!", which comes from exclusive familism, makes it difficult to find a sense of social responsibility or consideration of burden sharing with them. Regular surveys by the Korean Research Institute show that only 45% supported a proposal to add financial assistance to the victims of social distancing such as small business owners, the self-employed, and nonregular workers, while 72% supported it in Japan (Chun, 2020.12.22). Even though the New World Church and Love First Church were blamed as sources of the disease spread, it is difficult to find any social inclination to consider or sympathize with the fact that denouncing them could violate the right of church members to worship face-to-face. It has been apathetic to the freedom of assembly and association that the people should enjoy by justifying blocking or denouncing protests, asking for President Moon's resignation, and demonstrations, organized by the Korean Federation of Trade Union, as disease prevention efforts. These churches and protesters are also insensitive to their responsibility to the entire society outside of their own communities while they insist on their own inward-oriented interests or rights.

One of the reasons why the government, which has boasted of its achievements in protection from disease as "K-protection", was flustered by responding late in securing vaccines, which are considered one of the fastest means to do away with COVID-19, is that securing vaccines seems retrograde to the framework of exclusive familism, which provides the most differential treatment to those outside of one's own community. Vaccines run directly counter to the spirit of "No one pushes me around" since vaccines are used to end the disease by promoting immunity throughout the whole social community.

Therefore, the tendency to extend responsibility to other people is also expanded and reproduced due to social distancing, results in the blocking of information from others outside the family as it limits the living boundaries to individuals or families, and consequently blocks the sharing of balanced information. Despite having contact with external sources through information and communication devices such as the Internet, there is an echo chamber effect since the feedback is selective; the only information chosen is information that affirms the existing order. In other words, it amplifies preconceived convictions and beliefs. At the level of group dynamics, this results in a group extremization phenomenon (Choi et al., 2020, pp. 254–255). While expanding and reproducing the established order, people build a wall of prejudice and shut themselves up in their own caves. This again leads to the mass production of extreme fandom, which is no different from the deepening of exclusive familism.

Most importantly, even if there are contradictions and conflicts within the relationship between government and civil society and between the government's strategy of controlling disease and civil society itself, there is within civil society the desire to put them aside and avoid direct confrontations. In a social crisis, exclusive familism has a tendency to set aside any contradictions and flaws inherent in the social system outside of one's family. In a crisis, there is no reason to deal with the whole system since it is not a problem for oneself or one's own family. Therefore, focusing only on an imminent crisis requires the wisdom of maintaining the current system to reduce further disruptions or risks. Since we call it a "mentality of system justification" (Chun, 2020.06.12), a tendency to accept and support the government's response grows for time being. In other words, the desire to overcome the crisis increases, maintaining the current system rather than improving it (Chun, 2020.06.12). It is why the ruling party's victory in the 21st National Assembly election on April 15, 2020, with more than two-thirds of all seats, should be interpreted as a result of a passive response to minimize the risk of power transfer and dispersion rather than as a sign of active confidence in the government. The ruling party's victory means a result of forced choice and not a voluntary evaluation or choice (Chun, 2020.06.12). It is an outcome where fear from the uncertainty and ambiguity of the disease have overwhelmed distrust in the government.

3. Meritocracy and contract state frame

As the crisis becomes more routinized, the transition of the family state to a contract state intensified. This is why cooperative or passive governance becomes mainstream. The consciousness of the family state, which counts me, my neighbors, and the entire social community as a group bound by a common destiny, restored trust in the government and strengthened the penetration power of the state, working as a complement to the limitations of the contract state as a flat state. This is confirmed by the overall high level of trust in the government in research conducted after the spread of the COVID-19 pandemic (Chun, 2020.06.12). Seen from the perspective of the contract state, this means that the state has come to the fore in protecting the safety and health of its people, which can be regarded as a commitment to the people.

As a result, the following achievements were made: the cumulative number of tests as of December 2020 was 4,753,278 and that of isolated cases was 1,138,461. The volunteers working on site consisted of 2,509 doctors, 3,327 nurses, and 907 nursing staff. Also, 2,431 cases were confirmed by entry screening at airports, and 1,567 cases were confirmed by provisional screening clinics. The effectiveness of the administration in preventing infectious disease revealed in this process was also high. While the ratio of confirmed cases to examined cases was 70% in Egypt, South Korea maintained about 1%, and the fatality rate, indicating the death rate compared to confirmed cases, was only 2% in comparison with the large number of European countries such as the UK, France, Italy, Belgium, and the Netherlands, showing more than 10% (Moon, 2020a, p. 43).

The 4-T strategy worked well to achieve such outcomes. First, regarding diagnostic **test** activities, diagnostic kits were developed quickly beginning in mid-January, when the gene sequencing of COVID-19 was secured. This was possible because, as a result of the lessons learned from the MERS situation, the KCDC and the Ministry of Food and Drug Safety (MFDS) expedited approval procedures. Through the emergency use approval system, the diagnosis kit approval period, which normally takes about 80 days, was reduced to one week. Given the rapid diffusion of COVID-19, it was important to respond quickly, and it does not need to be mentioned that diagnosis is the first effective tool to realize such a deterrent policy. Securing a diagnostic kit means that a control tool against the virus was secured.

To increase the favorable social response to diagnosis, it was also effective to install various forms of innovative screening centers in neighborhoods along with a wide range of free tests. The various ideas suggested by doctors at diagnostic test sites were immediately accepted by the government and initiated throughout the country. Drive-throughs, walk-throughs, and open walk-throughs are typical examples (Wee, 2020, p. 11). The United States, Japan, Canada, Germany and the Netherlands introduced drive-throughs, and the United States, India, and Israel adopted the walk-through system from South Korea. Thus K-prevention of infectious disease began to be regarded as a symbol of leadership in the global response to COVID-19.

In the sense that the implementation of diagnosis activities requires on-the-spot services, a regional response strategy was adopted in connection with local autonomous governments. With at least one health center in every city district and county, a total of 254 installations went up across the country within eight days after the first case was confirmed to provide close and decentralized access to the sites. This reflects the disease response capability of local governments and the soundness of calling in local communities (No. 2020, p. 33).

Through such diagnosis systems, the spread of COVID-19 was controlled by quickly **tracing** and isolating confirmed cases without having to isolate any specific areas or restrict movement. By fusing information and communication devices and epidemiological investigations, the movements of confirmed cases were tracked by tracing cellular phone locations, the history of credit card and transportation card use, CCTV data, dashcam information, and QR codes. For isolated people, a system also monitored them through apps connected with a doctor when deemed necessary or warning them to immediately return to quarantine by sounding a smartphone alarm when they left a designated location. The systems tracked and monitored people so quickly and accurately that they came to be the world's leading means of epidemiological investigation of infectious diseases. This was possible because the experience of the MERS outbreak paved the way to enable people to provide the information necessary for epidemiological investigations and to oblige mobile and card companies to comply with the demands of the authorities per the Law on the Prevention and Control of Infectious Diseases. However, in the case of communication location data, the information was made available through the approval of the police in accordance with the Act on the Protection, Use, Etc. of Location Information. To this end, a cloud-based online epidemiological investigation support system was developed. The local governments were granted the right to disclose information related to unspecified individuals through social networks in order to trace the movements of confirmed cases. They adopted a strategy to prevent and control infectious disease for the entire community, even at the risk of violating the privacy of citizens and some private property rights (So, 2020, p. 60). Such tracking investigation was possible owing much to the high penetration rate of smartphones, the ability to collect and utilize data, and the dedicated efforts of the KCDC, along with a systematic business cooperation system between mobile and card companies, and active cooperation and collaboration among the Ministry of Land, Infrastructure and Transport, the Ministry of Science and ICT, the Ministry of Health and Welfare, and the Board of Audit and Inspection (S. Kim, 2020, p. 73).

Regarding **treatment**, people experienced confusion due to poor medical access and lack of medical treatment systems during the initial stage of the New World Church situation in Daegu City. However, thanks to a dedicated medical staff and excellent medical care, they were able to overcome this and reduce their need to sacrifice. By accepting the concept of a residential treatment center proposed by medical staff, they also were able to respond to a shortage of hospital beds. Treatment facilities were installed and operated for asymptomatic cases and mild symptom cases for which isolation treatment was not urgently requested, and thus they were treated in external facilities rather than in hospitals. This reduced the number of critical patients waiting to be admitted and created an environment where patients could be treated in time. There were 16 government-run residential treatment centers, including four locations under the direct supervision of the Central Disaster Management Headquarters and 12 local government organizations nationwide, with an accommodation capacity of 3,478 patients and 2,168 admitted people as of November 30, 2020 (Shin, 2020.12.02).

The overall therapeutic performance of the confirmed cases was also high. This is largely because of the contributions of the medical staff and government officials concerned. Overtime work was routine, but all of them endured it. It was no different from a wartime culture that responds to crisis situations. The experience gained from the MERS outbreak in 2015 also greatly contributed. Although not well-known to the general public, as a result of reflection on the response to the MERS outbreak, the expansion of negative pressure rooms and the reinforcement of epidemic intelligence (service) officers (EIS/EI officers), strengthening the civilian cooperation system for the development of diagnostic kits, the stockpiling of essential medical supplies, the development of response manuals, etc. were made (Moon, 2020a, p. 44). Among other things, developed medical facilities, medical technology, and the national health insurance system have worked as a foundation for high therapeutic performance. The highest innovative medical welfare system among the OECD member nations has minimized the burden on patients' medical expenses while being more accessible and efficient, resulting in higher satisfaction.

However, understanding that the foundation of all this response was to secure **trust** between the government and the people, various efforts were made to do so. Recalling that the situation worsened when the health authorities failed in crisis management communication with the public during the MERS outbreak in 2015, they tried to gain social trust in the authorities by providing accurate and transparent information about the moving routes of confirmed cases and the virus (Park, 2020, pp. 37–38). As the perception that government-provided information was reliable proliferated, trust in the government increased, and the effect of blocking fake news or rumors

COVID-19 response implementation governance 41

related to COVID-19 was also manifested. Two daily briefings worked as an effective tool to increase social trust in the KCDC, and the disaster text messaging services had the effect of giving people the belief that it was controlling the disaster situation well. This has brought about as an outcome of positively changing the perceptions of the social system and of the state as well (Choi et al., 2020, p. 222).

Needless to say, the most efficient factor contributing to the increase in public trust in the government is the accumulation of visible achievements in disease prevention efforts. Public trust in the government increased as the achievements of controlling infectious disease accumulated, owing much to the contribution of the family state as a manifestation of crisis consciousness and its subsequent outcomes at the initial stage, and a passive governance between civil society and the state was thereby formed after the Middle period, resulting in a change that expanded the scope of approval in reserving individual freedom from the state. This phenomenon of a surplus in trust in the government was confirmed by the increase in the number of people who felt confidence in the government's messages or increased trust in the government after its response to COVID-19. It also gave birth to a chain of trust reactions to the role of the public. In addition, it has had a positive effect on the self-esteem of South Koreans. With COVID-19, 65.1% of the people felt that South Korea had advanced more than other countries. Even in a situation that is bound to increase anxiety, owing much to the nature of the tasks concerned, the government's clear and rapid sharing of information enabled people to quench it (Choi et al., 2020, p. 204).

Notes

1 The degree of severity was measured by the responses "it's very serious" and "serious" to the question, "How serious do you think the domestic spread of COVID-19 is?"
2 The degree of positiveness of the government response was counted by adding the responses "doing very well" and "generally doing well" to the question, "How do you think the president and the government are responding to the COVID-19 crisis?"

5 Outcomes of COVID-19 response implementation governance

1. Family state and social capital

From a close-up view of South Korea's COVID-19 response over the past year, it is seen that a variety of forms of governance have taken place, interacting between the perceptional framework of family state that counts families as a basic unit of social composition and that of the contract state that treats individuals as the units of social composition. At the beginning of the outbreak, the response was passive governance of which the contract state led family state, and as newly confirmed cases increased, the response was cooperative governance, in which the contract state and family state collaborated with each other in similar proportions. However, as the situation did not improve, it changed to proactive governance in which a nervous family state came to the front of the contract state. As the crisis subsided, they explored cooperative governance again and replaced it with passive governance as the situation further stabilized. This situation remained the same for quite some time, but when the number of newly confirmed cases showed signs of a rebound, they responded with cooperative governance and shifted back to passive governance as the situation stabilized. When the newly confirmed cases increased, they switched to cooperative governance, and when the situation rapidly worsened, they responded with proactive governance again. As the crisis subsided, they went back to cooperative governance and showed a shift in response to passive governance. Such a series of situational changes took place until November 25, 2020, when the data were last collected.

One of the characteristics that we can learn from this is that the contract state, which has been evaluated as relatively lacking state power or control over the situation, and the flat state, which is the concrete manifestation of it, have demonstrated their ability to respond to the crisis fairly effectively. According to the international journal *Nature*, as of September 1, 2020, 5% of the 3.4 billion people in 45 countries were infected with the coronavirus, South Korea had the lowest rate of coronavirus infection with 0.06%, while

DOI: 10.4324/9781003240709-5

Peru in South America had the highest rate of infection (Lee, 2020.11.03). It is believed that the lack of social support and trust, which can be said to be the weak point of the flat state, was supplemented by the family state, noting that such an achievement was made despite of the fact that passive governance has been maintained for most of the past year. This is because the phenomenon of the switching state was triggered, bringing in the sense of the family state peculiar to South Korean society, owing much to the understanding that the country was in crisis, unlike usual times. This is also confirmed by the fact that the number of newly confirmed cases is declining as the family state comes to the fore, shifting passive or cooperative governance to proactive governance whenever the situation becomes serious. Therefore, the success factor of South Korea's prevention of infectious disease, to which the world is paying attention, comes from the consciousness of the family state unique to South Korean society.

Noting that the family state is an epistemological framework of civic engagement, it can be regarded as a unique social capital of South Korean society. Similarly, Chun (2020.06.02) presents "democratic civility" as a prime factor leading to the success of South Korea's COVID-19 prevention and control. However, the basic unit of democratic civility is different from that of the family state. Democratic civility, which has been regarded in the West as the basis for social stability and democratic government, makes individuals a basic unit of social composition. They are assumed to respond with cold and rational judgments and reasonable choices. Therefore, in the real world of its operation, it is easy to fall into individual-centered selfishness, and it opts to be exposed to an imbalance that enjoys rights but does not have corresponding obligations. To overcome this, the cold relationship schema such as laws and contracts is not enough, and it is bound to require community commitment (Choi, 1999, p. 24). The family state stands in contrast to democratic civility in that it emphasizes and is driven by emotional and sensible solidarity through dedication and sacrifice.

The family state is also different from the "social capital" that Putnam (1995) or Fukuyama (1997) have presented. Putnam (1995) saw that networks, norms and social trust are required to promote the coordination and cooperation needed to increase mutual benefits for the members of a society. Because the basic units of social composition are regarded as individuals, in order to fulfill aspirations, the self-interest of each individual must be prioritized, and there has to be coordination and compromise among them. Therefore, networks, norms, and social trust are counted as essential components to minimize the conversion costs that come with the process. However, since the consciousness of the family state looks at the whole society of a nation as a family, speaks of commitment and contribution to it and tries to realize by itself instead of going through the conversion process, it is fundamentally different in its mechanisms of operation, even if they are alike in the sense that they both aim for social integration and unity. In particular, Fukuyama (1997) separated societies into "high-trust societies" and "low-trust societies" and reviewed how trust is related to politics, economy, society, and culture. He saw South Korea as one of the leading low-trust societies and found the cause in Korean familism. It is said that, under familism, all social life is made up of families as a basic unit, whereby individuals seek identity, belonging, and interests, and they do not trust individuals or groups beyond the scope of family. As a result, he said, a high level of trust is formed within the family, but society as a whole has a low level of trust, which is considered a vulnerable factor for economic and social development. Therefore, he expressed a view that the accumulation of social capital is essential for a low-trust country such as South Korea to achieve economic development and political democratization and that it must overcome a social culture that emphasizes hierarchical order and the family culture of Confucianism. It is no different from arguing that the negative effects of exclusive familism should be overcome. However, this view overlooks the fact that not only emotional familism but also exclusive familism can serve not only as a positive driver for overcoming crises, such as promoting social distancing and wearing masks, in the daily lives of infectious disease prevention and control but also in promoting social cohesion and reducing conversion costs, especially during a social crisis. After all, in that sense, Fukuyama's theory of a low-trust society is no different from evaluating South Korean familism on the bases of Western prejudices.

2. Switching state and contextual governance

Needless to say, we need trusted state leadership to manage government efficiently. This is absolutely necessary, especially in the circumstances of a pan-social crisis such as COVID-19. This is because trust in government leaders is a key factor in determining whether the state and civil society can cooperate efficiently (Kauzya, 2020, p. 4). But this is half right and half wrong. It is true that since social trust in the leadership and civil society in their response to the state are in a positive proportional relationship, the higher the social trust to the state is, the higher the degree of civil society's response and cooperation with the leadership of the state will be, increasing the possibility of forming cooperative governance. The reverse relationship is also available. The lower the degree of trust in the state there is, the less likely it is to form cooperative governance. The more such a situation is likely to be manifested, the lower the severity of crisis is. If the severity of crisis situations decreases and reaches an ordinary state, and the trust in the state is low, the civil society's response to the state becomes relatively low.

It is a case that the laissez-faire type of governance explains well. However, when the severity of crisis situations is high, things become different. When the degree of trust in the state is low in comparison with the severity of a crisis, civil society does not simply stand by or show a low degree of favorable response. As we see in the case of proactive governance, civil society may lead the state and actively work to overcome crisis situations. No, the greater the distrust to the state is, the more positive and proactive civil society's response to crisis situations becomes.

This was evident in South Korea's response to COVID-19 for the prevention and control of infectious disease. In situations where the severity of crisis is high and trust to the state is relatively low, proactive governance led by civil society works to ameliorate crisis situations. As proactive governance is working at critical moments of changing from the Former period to the Middle period and from the Middle period to the Latter period of COVID-19 outbreak, civil society is preventing society from deepening to crisis. There are not a few explanations for the high level of trust that South Korea's government enjoys in the implementation of infectious disease prevention and control policies was a key factor in its success in responding to COVID-19 (Klingebiel & Tørres, 2020, p. 4). But you must ask where that trust comes from. In particular, before entering a crisis, the South Korean government as a flat state has always experienced a trust deficit. We must find what external factors outside of government strengthened the power of the vulnerable state and its policy implementation capability as it entered the crisis. In that respect, the frame of the family state is not much different from an appealing explanation variable.

Such a change has been manifested by the switching state phenomenon peculiar to South Korean society. In South Korea, the perceptional framework of governance is reversed from a contract state to a family state when things are deemed to be serious. This is possible because traditional familism not only makes the boundaries between public and private arenas unclear but also results in changes that absorb the contract state as the boundaries of the family state expand with fluidity. It means that, in favor of the family state, it is loosely coupled with the contract state. It is no different from talking about the advent of proactive governance.

Therefore, in the early stages of governance formation, it becomes important to determine the extent of the crisis or the nature of the context. However, the general theory of governance is not yet sophisticated enough to deal with such issues. Reviewing the literature of governance theories, governance is understood as an epistemological framework from which science and politics converge and the state and civil society interact through endogenous dialectics (Carmel, 2019; Fawcett & Daugbjerg, 2012) or as a legal dimension from which the substance of law and system are identified (Eom,

2012; Kornhauser, 2004), as a behavioral dimension that is understood as a form of decision-making process (Gorgulhoa et al., 2015; Maharaj, 2009), and as a form of service delivery when it is observed at the front line (Irene, 2018; Ahmad, 2008) to grasp the major perspectives generally. However, there is a lack of discussion about going through a strategic judgment of weighing and considering whether the state and civil society should build cooperative relations with each other prior to establishing such governance relations, about the question of how much binding power should be pursued if they are to be built, about whether the movement from government to governance is inevitable, and about whether the state and civil society should be coupled to each other and with how much intensity if they are so required. When we refer to such a step of strategic judgement as contextual governance, we must add contextual governance phase to the existing theoretical discussions about governance.[1]

3. Dual state and cultural approach

A dual state, where the family state and the contract state coexist as in South Korea, can generally be divided into a hybrid dual state, where the two are mixed, and a switching dual state, where one side overwhelms the other at some point. The former can be found in the theoretical framework of the dual economy developed by Lewis (1965). The theory of a dual economy would see the gap and duality between urban industrial areas and rural agricultural areas as a core determining factor of underdevelopment. For the other, there is a theory of the dual state by Morgenthau (1962). According to him, the regular state hierarchy, which operates according to rule of law, is visible in the United States on the one hand, while on the other hand, there is a security hierarchy behind it that monitors it. So that if a security crisis is identified that is serious enough to limit the democratic political process, Morgenthau has seen that real veto power is exercised over the decisions made by the regular state hierarchy as it comes to the front.

Until now, most of the theoretical discussions have rated the dual state as unreasonable, dysfunctional and an obstacle to development because they have taken hybrid dual states for granted and developed discussions therefrom. It is a representative evaluation that traditional culture and norms collide with the rule of law in modern society, bringing confusion to decision making and leading to underdevelopment. However, it owes much to the facts that the relationship between the family state and the contract state has built a switching dual state and not a hybrid dual state and that the dual state in South Korea has played a positive role in efficiently responding to crises, such as the prevention and control of COVID-19. In particular, in response to crisis, the emergence of a switching state, where the family state overshadowed by the contract state comes to front, has brought positive effects to the efficient control and prevention of infectious disease.

Among these, cooperative governance, in which the family state and the contract state intervene with a similar weight, is likely to be accompanied by similar problems to those of the hybrid dual state. Cooperative governance implies that the family state and the contract state are not biased toward either side and rather reflect balanced political preferences and professional judgments. In that respect, it could be considered closest to the needs of democratic polity, but in actual operation it is not only a difficult request to manifest but also therefore includes normative and prescriptive restraining factors. When the two sides look for a balance, since neither side can overwhelm the other, there is no small possibility that the time consumed in coordinating each other's positions and the costs of learning required to coordinate different opinions could work as negative factors in a time of crisis management that requires a rapid response. This means that proactive governance or passive governance, in which either side takes the lead in responding to crisis, is rather advantageous.

However, approaching it from a historical and cultural perspective, the relationship between the family state and the contract state forming a dual state is no different from the phenomenon of "the simultaneity of the non-simultaneous". Bloch (1977) saw that premodernity in the era of Prussian authoritarianism and modern liberal democracy, represented by the Weimar Constitution, coexisted at the present time in the political culture of Germany during the Weimar period and that this phenomenon of "the simultaneity of the non-simultaneous" occurs not only in multiple time dimensions but also in multiple space dimensions. In South Korea, the juxtaposition of Western modernity with non-Western premodernity at the same time has been counted as the starting point of social conflicts and the root cause of all kinds of evils. However, it has been proved by the COVID-19 response process that the epistemological frame of premodernity could be an efficient alternative to solving the problems of the real world when they take the form of the switching state by being released from the equal bonding between Western modernity and non-Western premodernity and loosely coupled or decoupled. This is because the family state, a legacy of premodernity, has worked as a key changer that complements the limits of the contract state as a flat state. While Western individualism has worked as a key factor in neutralizing communitarianism, such as not cooperating by wearing a mask, in South Korea, premodern familial fraternity and bonding have worked as a base for easily accepting the responsibilities for bearing the cost required to maintain communitarianism. It can be noted that "the simultaneity of the non-simultaneous" works as a key component of the switching state, that is, to apply the time variable differentially. Approaching this from the perspective of familism as a legacy of traditional culture, it serves to highlight the importance of cultural variables in crisis response governance.

From this point of view, state capacity, people's trust and leadership etc., which were pointed out by Fukuyama (2020) as the determining factors in the successful prevention and control of infectious disease, may be necessary but not sufficient conditions. This is because family state consciousness works as a determining factor for a successful response in South Korea. Therefore, we cannot help paying attention to the importance of cultural variables. From this perspective, some look for the factors of South Korea's success in the prevention of infectious disease from the authoritarian and top-down hierarchical system, but this is nothing but an error that is made from superficial observations of Confucian familism. Even though the viewpoint is based on Confucianism, it is more appropriate to understand the family state of South Korea with its focus on emotional commitment and sacrifice among family members.

Therefore, it is not easy for other countries to replicate these factors since the success of South Korea's quarantine owes much to the unique cultural heritage of its society. Even though it is often evaluated in terms of the effectiveness of the 4-T strategy of test, trace, treatment and trust, it would have been difficult for all of the T's to play their roles if the family state consciousness peculiar to South Korean society had not supported them. By the same logic, it is never easy to transplant or replicate in other countries facing crisis situations the sense of the switching state that has been accumulated through frequent experiences of war, as it operates as a driving force for the transition to the family state. That is why the research that approaches crisis response implementation governance from a cultural perspective should be expanded further in the wake of the COVID-19 crisis (He et al., 2020, p. 254).

4. Information society and proactive governance

Crisis situations caused by structural contradictions cannot be responded to efficiently by only the contract state that relies on rational and reasonable judgments, scientism and rule of law. The meaning of a crisis situation itself is no different from the implication that the government's ability to respond to such situations has reached its inherent limits. Therefore, it means a situation that cannot be managed unilaterally by the state and that requires supplementation by other dimensions of ruling mechanisms such as decentralization, public and private partnerships, and civic engagement. Such a situation is intensified further as we move from a solid society to a liquid society. As the structure of a solid society, which emphasizes order and rule of law, collapses and changes to a more fluid and dynamic state, the role of government that relies on monism, rule of law, and preemptive response becomes more likely to be vulnerable. In a rapidly changing and fluid society of networks, it becomes inevitable to rely on the flow of communication, as the structure, which guarantees the stability of meaning and identity, collapses and changes rapidly. It means that the source of authority also becomes pluralized.

These changes cannot help but increase the importance of demands on the role of civil society, particularly because the capability of civil society is different from in the past. Ever since the advent of the information society, individuals who make up civil society have become further able to take control, judge and react to social phenomena much more efficiently than before. A typical example is that communication flow and sharing and the spread of information among individuals have become more rapid and accurate. All of the 4-T strategies attempted by the contract state in connection with the COVID-19 response were supported by information and communication devices. The vulnerable penetration power of the flat state has been supported and expanded by these information and communication technologies. This owes much, of course, to the revolutionary improvement of each person's ability to manage information in connection with such information and communication devices. As the source of authority becomes diversified, a social environment has been achieved in which no one can impose their own unilateralism. This is possible because, in South Korea, the information society has already become routinized.

Such an information society also drives the movement of power between the state and civil society. It has been understood that the governance relationship is generally formulated in the process of transferring government power to civil society or sharing it with civil society ever since the advent of the neoliberal system. However, the relationship between the state and civil society revealed in the COVID-19 response is not a phenomenon that occurs in the process of transferring authority, penetration power or jurisdiction of the flat state to civil society. It stems from the strengthening of autonomous self-controlling power that is generated by itself within civil society. It differs from the theories of governance that have been discussed on the bases of the existing philosophical background of neoliberalism, in the sense that it did not originate from the revival of preexisting suffrage but from the creation of a new one. This is because it speaks of exerting its own self-help and spontaneous role, which is self-generated, regardless of the already existing role of the state. Nor is it caused by replacing hierarchy with a network or by converting centralized state power into decentralized governance. However, in the case of South Korea, the complementary role of civil society arises from the situation where we cannot confirm that an overbureaucratized system with strong penetration power is already established.

It is more than that. Governance seeks to promote bilateral interaction, cooperation or supportive relations on the premise of the concept of a binary boundary between state and civil society. However, the family state, on the other end, presupposes that the boundary between state and civil society is not only unclear but also continues to flow. While governance assumes a delegation of authority and responsibility between the state and civil society or market, the family state is no different from a form of liquid democracy in the sense that it adjusts its boundaries and converges with the contract state. While most of the governances are built on the ideological legitimacy of neoliberalism, the family state is close to inclusive governance. It does not mean an extension of the small government theories but a part of the work of democratization, not a simple resurgence of preexisting participatory power but a new creation and expansion of it. As it speaks to the composition of governance through competition and cohesion, it requires more critical evaluation and interpretation when we see it from the perspective of traditional governance theories.

5. Success of crisis response and overcoming Western cultural bias

Koreans evaluate themselves as having successfully responded to COVID-19. As Figure 4-1 shows, according to 20 surveys conducted by the Korean Research Institute in 2020 (Lee, 2020.11.25), the responses evaluating whether the government was responding to COVID-19 positively ran, on average, at an annual rate of 71.6%. Objective indicators such as the development rate of the disease and the case fatality rate (CFR) also prove this. However, it was the active and positive evaluations from the outside world that made a significant contribution to this positive self-conviction.

The U.S. daily newspaper *The Wall Street Journal* (2020.09.25) cited South Korea as the country that responded best to COVID-19. In the early days of the pandemic, the paper said, South Korea had suppressed virus transmission better than other developed countries around the world and twice as effectively as the United States and the United Kingdom. It also said that the economic growth forecast of South Korea is −0.8% in 2020, which is the best economic indicator among OECD member countries. Meanwhile, the rest of world continues to suffer from the COVID-19 crisis (Kang, 2020.09.26). The U.S. economic magazine *Forbes* (2020.09.30), citing a research report by the Hong Kong–based think tank Deep Knowledge Group (DKG), reported, "South Korea is the third most safe among 100 safe countries in the COVID-19 crisis". The report evaluated safety of economy, politics, health and health care related to COVID-19 in 250 countries. First place went to Germany and second place to New Zealand

(Nam, 2020.09.18). Bloomberg Communications (2020.10.23) published a COVID-19 recovery index form and said that South Korea ranked fourth among 53 countries with a gross domestic product (GDP) of more than $200 billion. The index is a comprehensive score of ten indicators related to the COVID-19 situation and quality of life, including infections per 100,000 people per month, vaccine accessibility, freedom of movement and GDP outlook (Kim, 2020.11.25).

Such positive evaluations by the global village not only provided a momentum to make K-quarantine a national brand but also contributed greatly to upgrading its global image. It has contributed greatly to the strengthening of soft power by innovatively increasing the visibility of South Korea in the international community. This has also brought a change where K-quarantine itself is used as a concrete and practical means of diplomatic cooperation (Klingebiel & Tørres, 2020, p. 8).

Such evaluations by the global community that the government of South Korea responded to COVID-19 with great success have provided an opportunity to increase the pride of South Koreans to their own government innovatively (Choi et al., 2020, p. 224). According to a poll reported on June 2, 2020, 11% of people think that South Koreans tended to divide easily after the outbreak of the COVID-19 pandemic, while 64% have changed their minds and thought that they "tend to unite well" (Chun, 2020.06.02). Even more noteworthy is that 43% of the responders confirmed that "I have been led to believe that the taxes I pay are spent properly", nearly double the 24% who believed that "the taxes are wasted". (Chun, 2020.06.02). This means that there has been a significant increase in the belief that the contract state is functioning properly in the era of COVID-19. Even with regard to tax administration, it's generally hard to find cases where people's credibility has risen, but such rare cases have occurred. It is assessed that the crisis response by the contract state was evaluated as effective.

More importantly, these changes have led to overcoming the complex of developed countries. When asked to compare the capabilities of developed countries to those of South Korea in responding to COVID-19, 39% said that South Korea was better than the developed countries in its overall capabilities, and 31% said they were similar. Combining both of the responses, 70% thought that South Korea had reached the level of developed countries (Chun, 2020.06.02). The evaluation of the competency of ordinary citizens is more generous: 84% rated the capabilities of South Korean citizens as ahead of or not much different from those of developed countries (Chun, 2020.06.02). This change means that South Korea has overcome the perennial complex of feeling like a deficient state, a needy state, a vulnerable state, a frozen state, of feeling that it has suffered for a long time and sees itself with new eyes filled with self-esteem. For the first time ever in South

Korea's modern history, this vision correction has led the country to place itself as one of the leading countries in the global community. Above all, it is now able to look at itself neutrally, overcoming the sense of Western civilization's supremacy.

Note

1 In a review of the literature, contextual governance has been treated as a governance either in different cultural backgrounds (OECD, 2013) or in different organizational characteristics (Zainon et al., 2013). And seldom has it been researched as a governance in different work environments such as a crisis.

6 Conclusion

The government of South Korea as a flat state, which is usually rated as vulnerable in its penetration power in society, has achieved remarkable results in its COVID-19 response, and such a success is believed to owe much to a combination of environmental factors such as crisis situations, familism that is a unique cultural characteristic of South Korean society, and the characteristics of an information society. Among these, familism is nothing but a key factor that has driven the active response of civil society in shaping the implementation governance in response to the COVID-19 outbreak.

In Western society, it goes without saying that the populace requests the contract state to respond to crisis, to which the suffrage of individuals is entrusted in the assumption that it will take the responsibility for safeguarding and protecting the people in the face of crises. Therefore, how highly such states and central governments enjoy trust from the people is also one of the key indicators and drivers of success in the process of responding to crisis. However, under the frame of the family state, which understands the state as an extension of the family, as in South Korea, the more they face crisis, the more they think that they cannot simply wait and leave it to the state since the state is like a family in a broad sense, prioritizing the consciousness that it is not a matter for me and for my family as well. It is why civil society is responding to crisis more proactively and preemptively. Therefore, the condition of a state trust deficit rather functions as one of the key factors that instigates a proactive response by civil society.

Under this framework of perception, all agile governance and evidence-based governance or resilient governance and adaptive governance, which have been evaluated as necessary to overcome crisis situations such as COVID-19, simply presuppose conversion costs and try to reduce the costs incurred in that process. However, more fundamentally, it goes without saying that it is faster and more efficient when civil society responds and recovers on its own by minimizing or circumventing the transition process

DOI: 10.4324/9781003240709-6

without going through the government. In particular, in situations where medical science–oriented responses such as therapeutics and prophylactic drugs are not available, as with COVID-19, the citizens themselves are the starting point of infection and the diffusion host and furthermore can only be the subject of quarantine activities. For this matter, it is no wonder that civil society should be given greater weight. From this perspective, the fact that the family state of South Korea has played a key, preemptive, and proactive role in the operational process of COVID-19 crisis response implementation governance is no different from confirming that civil society has played a major role in the nation's successful response.

However, environmental factors such as crisis situations also worked as an important factor in compelling the family state play a leading role in responding to the crisis. Judging a situation as a serious crisis is a determining factor in making the family state more proactive and step forward from being juxtaposed between the contract state, as an administrative state responsible for safety and protection of the people, and the family state, which operates on the basis of emotional solidarity and commitment, in favor of the contract state. In that respect, it is thought that the general discussions about governance should now be extended to the governance dimension that deals with the issue of judging the nature of the context in which governance takes place, such as whether it is a crisis or not.

In addition, it has been common until now to discuss implementation governance within the boundaries of a nation because it presupposes an administrative state that operates on the base of national sovereignty within the borders of a nation. As a result, the variables outside a nation were not properly regarded as actors influencing the operation of implementation governance. However, in South Korea's response to COVID-19, the global community's judgment and evaluation that South Korea's response to COVID-19 was very successful and played a leading role worked as one of the main factors that increased public trust in the government. It is a reminder that there is a rising call for developing more systematic discussions on feedback governance, owing greatly to the facts that COVID-19 is a major contemporary issue for all members of the global community and that the elimination of obstacles in information communications arising from the advent of the information society is a key environmental factor related to that need. Of course, it is not an exaggeration to say that discussions about governance as a cooperative mutual assistance system between the state and civil society have not yet been extended to feedback governance. The challenge of improving this is one of the tasks left to researchers to come.

The dual state, in which the family state, left behind as a legacy of traditional social systems, is juxtaposed with the contract state in the modern sense, as in South Korea, has often been evaluated as a trigger for inefficiency and being uneconomic. From the perspective of modern scientism, which values economies of scale and rational and reasonable approaches, the dual state, in which emotional and affective factors are juxtaposed with rational and scientific factors seems to be evaluated as nothing more than a root cause of its own inefficiency and uneconomic functioning. In that respect, it is difficult to dispute the assessment that the dual state is the source of social dysfunctions arising from "the simultaneity of the non-simultaneous". However, in a crisis, it implies that there is a need to review whether the assessments of a dual state that have been raised so far have been accompanied by any Western bias, confirming the fact that the phenomenon of a dual state works rather as an efficient alternative to overcome crisis.

Considering that all the modern administrative states in the West, based on theories of the social contract and individualism, were not efficient in their COVID-19 response governance, it has provided an opportunity for South Korean society to review whether it has fallen into a Western culture supremacy complex. Although there have been discussions in the nation's intelligence community to seek South Korean standards after the advent of postmodernism, the requests for Korean standards of this time were only demands for a domestic response to the needs arising from the history of civilization and more specifically from the retreat of the modern framework within Western society. One of the additional but very important changes that has resulted from the recovery of self-esteem in South Korean society based on its successful response to COVID-19 is that, based on such pride, the self-consciousness needed to set South Korean standards according to the measures on which domestic society is judged and orders itself has been developed. That is no different from the self-reflection required to take the leap toward becoming a knowledge-producing country. To live so long as a knowledge-importing country meant that its ways of thinking were not independent but dependent. It was also one of the reasons why people still live in the logic of the camps preemptively divided (Choi, 2020.09.01), vying with one another for the supremacy of ideologies developed outside the country. The COVID-19 crisis, which has come to be one of the biggest global crises in the history of civilization, is paradoxically providing an opportunity for South Korean society to move away from such passive shackles.

Seen from the perspective of restored self-esteem, we can look back at the fact that most of the governance theories discussed so far have taken for granted that we should rely on the state to solve social problems. This is only an indicator that the need to devise a new alternative has become imminent, together with the reflection that the modern administrative state, which is the legacy of a solid state, is no longer an efficient alternative to solve social problems after the advent of the information society. This advent has been accompanied by changes that strengthen the penetration power of civil society in the relationship between the state and civil society, and it also functions as a factor to strengthen the autonomous activities of civil society. From the perspective that the information society has the property of strengthening vested interests by amplifying the existing social order, in Western society where a strong administrative state has worked, there is a high possibility that a state-friendly effect would likely take place in the relationship between the state and civil society. On the other hand, in a flat state where the penetration power of the state is relatively weak, as in South Korea, the possibility of operating for the expansion of an autonomous activity space of civil society becomes much greater. This was clearly evident in the response to COVID-19. Even though the government devised various forms of information and communication programs and responded with them, it was the active response by each individual citizen that really strengthened the autonomous activities of self-prevention and eventual control of disease on the base of the information they obtained. The paradox of the latecomer seems to be that the flat state of South Korea enjoys benefits and advantages and yet has failed to reach the level of the administrative state with its strong penetration power in the modern sense, as in the West.

References

Ahmad, R. (2008). Governance, social accountability and the civil society. *Journal of Administration & Governance, 3*(1), 10–21.

Bloch, E. (1977, [first published in German 1932]). Trans. Mark Ritter. Nonsynchronism and the obligation to its dialectics. *New German Critique, 11,* 22–38.

Boin, A., & Lodge, M. (2016). Designing resilient institutions for transboundary crisis management: A time for public administration. *Public Administration, 94*(2), 289–298.

Boswell, C., & Rodrigues, E. (2016). Policies, politics and organizational problems: Multiple streams and the implementation of targets in UK government. *Policy and Politics, 44*(4), 507–524.

Bowtell, B. (2020, March 6). Our HIV lesson: Exclude politicians and trust the experts-and the people-to confront coronavirus. *The Sydney Morning Herald.* Retrieved from www.smh.com.au/national/our-hiv-lesson-exclude-politicians-and-trust-the-experts-and-the-people-to-confront-coronavirus-20200305-p5476a.html

Brousselle, A., Brunet-Jailly, E., Kennedy, C., Phillips, S. D., Quigleym, K., & Roberts, A. (2020). Beyond COVID-19: Five commentaries on reimagining governance for future crises and resilience. *Canadian Public Administration, 63*(3), 369–408.

Carmel, E. (2019). Chapter 3: Governance analysis: Epistemological orientations and analytical framework. In E. Carmel (Ed.), *Governance analysis: Critical enquiry at the intersection of politics, policy and society.* Glos: Edward Elgar.

Center for Systems Science and Engineering (CSSE). (2020, December 30). *COVID-19 data repository.* Johns Hopkins University (JHU). Retrieved from www.google.co.kr/search?source=hp&ei=Vu3zX9iELsmnoATDn4fQBQ&q=%EC%BD%94%EB%A1%9C%EB%82%98+%EB%B0%94%EC%9D%B4%EB%9F%AC%EC%8A%A4+%EC%9D%BC%EC%9D%BC+%ED%99%95%EC%A7%84%EC%9E%90+%EC%88%98&oq=%EC%BD%94%EB%A1%9C%EB%82%98+%EC%9D%BC%EC%9D%BC+%ED%99%95%EC%A7%84%EC%9E%90+%EC%88%98&gs_lcp=CgZwc3ktYWIQARgBMgIIADIGCAAQCBAeMgYIABAIEB46BQgAELEDOgQIABAKOggIABCxAxCDAToGCAAQChAqOgcIABCxAxAKOgQIABADOggIABAIEA0QHlCDEVj3tgFgmJ0CaANwAHgDgAHcA4gBmlOSAQoxLjIuOC4zLjYuMy4ymAEAoAEBqgEHZ3dzLXdpeg&sclient=psy-ab

References

Choi, B. Y. (1997). *Confucian culture of the Chosun dynasty* (in Korean). Seoul: Four Seasons.

Choi, I. S., Yoon, D. H., Chae, S. A., & Song, E. T. (2020). *The power of reading and planning the public, 2021 trend monitor* (in Korean). Seoul: Secret House.

Choi, J. S. (2020, September 1). Prowinword-Japan and Republic of Korea. *Media Today* (in Korean). Retrieved from http://m.mediatoday.asia/181106#_enliple

Choi, J. U. (2017). *The discovery of Koreans: Finding the identity of power that moved Korean modern history* (in Korean). Seoul: Miji Books.

Choi, S. M. (1999). Theory composition and methodology for the bonding of Confucius ideas and democracy (in Korean). *Oriental Social Thoughts, 2*, 5–29.

Choi, W. Y. (2006). Chocun dynasty – changes in social relations and origins of familism (in Korean). Korean Association of Family Studies ed. *Family Culture, 18*(1), 1–32.

Choi, Y. J. (2008). The issue of governing actors and objects in the state theory of Confucianism (in Korean). *Oriental Philosophy Research, 53*, 145–175.

Chun, K. Y. (2020, June 2). Korean's world revealed by 'prevention and control of infectious disease politics' – unexpected responses (in Korean). *SisaIN*. Retrieved from www.sisain.co.kr/news/articleView.html?idxno=42132

Chun, K. Y. (2020, June 12). Korean's world revealed by 'prevention and control of infectious disease politics' – Koreans standing at crossroads (in Korean). *SisaIN*. Retrieved from www.sisain.co.kr/news/articleView.html?idxno=42165

Chun, K. Y. (2020, December 22). Korean's world revealed by 'prevention and control of infectious disease politics' – Koreans having doubts (in Korean). *SisaIN*. Retrieved from www.sisain.co.kr/news/articleView.html?idxno=43417

Chun, K. Y. (2021, January 4). Korean's world revealed by 'prevention and control of infectious disease politics' – warnings of 'no one back me up' (in Korean). *SisaIN*. Retrieved from www.sisain.co.kr/news/articleView.html?idxno=43617.

Cohen, M. D., March, J. G., & Olsen, J. P. (1972). A garbage can model of organizational choice. *Administrative Science Quarterly, 17*(1), 1–25.

Djalante, R. (2012). Adaptive governance and resilience: The role of multi-stakeholder platforms in disaster risk reduction. *Natural Hazards Earth System Sciences, 12*, 2923–2942.

Eom, S. J. (2012). Institutional dimensions of e-government development: Implementing the business reference model in the United States and Korea. *Administration & Society, 45*(7), 875–907.

Fawcett, P., & Daugbjerg, C. (2012). Explaining governance outcomes: Epistemology, network governance and policy network analysis. *Political Studies Review, 10*(2), 195–207.

Fukuyama, F. (1997). Social capital and the modern capitalist economy: Creating a high trust workplace. *Stern Business Magazine, 4*(1).

Fukuyama, F. (2004). The imperative of state-building. *Journal of Democracy, 15*(2), 17–31.

Fukuyama, F. (2020). The pandemic and political order: It takes a state. *Journal of Foreign Affairs, 99*, 4.

Giustiniano, L., Cunha, M. P. E., Simpson, A. V., Rego, A., & Clegg, S. (2020). Resilient leadership as paradox work: Notes from COVID-19. *Management and Organization Review, 16*(5), 971–975.

Gorgulhoa, J., Tavaresa, J., Páscoaa, C., & Tribolet, J. (2015). Governance: Decision-making model and cycle. *Procedia Computer Science, 64*, 578–585.

He, A. J., Shi, Y., & Liu, H. (2020). Crisis governance, Chinese style: Distinctive features of China's response to the COVID-19 pandemic. *Policy Design and Practice, 3*(3), 242–258.

Henderson, G. (1968). *Korea: The politics of the vortex* (p. 479). Cambridge, MA: Harvard University Press.

Hwang, K. S., Jung, I. J., Lee, S. H., Kim, H. C., Lee, K. D., Park, C. Y., . . . Lee, J. W. (1996). *Convergence of ethics order* (in Korean). Seoul: Philosophy and Reality Printing.

Irene, O. F. (2018). Enhancing governance and operational effectiveness of civil society organisations for quality service delivery in South Africa. *International Journal of Governance and Development, 5*, 47–52.

Janssen, M., & van der Voort, H. (2020). Agile and adaptive governance in crisis response: Lessons from the COVID-19 pandemic. *International Journal of Information Management, 55*, 1–7.

Jin, S. C. (2020, April 8). [Plague in history (1)] the Roman empire fallen by plague, a message from the history (in Korean). *The Epoch Times*.

Jung, J. K. (2020). The role of civil society in South Korean democracy: Liberal legacy and its pitfalls. In *Asia democracy issue briefing*. Seoul: The East Asia Institute.

Kang, G. T. (2020, September 26). WSJ "South Korea, COVID-19-response password unraveled" . . . K-prevention and control of infectious disease, a cover story (in Korean). *Yonhap News Agency*. Retrieved from www.yna.co.kr/view/AKR20200926005300072

Kang, M. G. (2007). What is not covered by the debate on liberalism? (In Korean) *People and Thought, 4*, 41–54.

Kauzya, J. M. (2020). *COVID-19: Reaffirming state-people governance relationships*. UN/DESA policy brief #75. Department of Economic and Social Affairs, UN.

Kim, D. C. (2020). *Korean's energy and familism* (in Korean). Seoul: Book Publishing Pierna.

Kim, D. H., & Cho, S. M. (2020). The dilemma of the mask policy in COVID-19 quarantine – partial dilemma response through KF-AD mask standards (in Korean). *Winter Conference Proceedings of the Korean Society of Public Administration, 2020*(1), 437–447.

Kim, E. H. (2018, December 8). Who are the gentry (*Yangban*)? (In Korean) (1). *Facebook*. Retrieved from www.facebook.com/eunhee.kim.79230/posts/2195112207200412.

Kim, E. H. (2020, July 9). Who are the gentry (*Yangban*)? (In Korean) (6). *Facebook*. Retrieved from www.facebook.com/eunhee.kim.79230/posts/3337548939623394

Kim, E. H. (2020, July 17). Who are the gentry (*Yangban*)? (In Korean) (6). *Facebook*. Retrieved from www.facebook.com/eunhee.kim.79230/posts/3360314690680152

Kim, J. D. (2020, November 25). 'Corona response capability,' If you are embarrassed to learn that Korea is behind Japan (in Korean). *Money Today*. Retrieved from https://news.mt.co.kr/mtview.php?no=2020112517401107562.

Kim, K. M. (2018). Korean political and economic model from a comparative perspective (in Korean). *Korean Political Studies, 27*(1), 375–402.

References

Kim, M. H. (2020). Public health crisis response and cooperative governance (in Korean). *Administrative Focus*, *146*, 69–71.

Kim, S. J. (2020). Data and corona 19, 4th industrial revolution and post-corona era (in Korean). *Administrative Focus*, *147*, 68–73.

Kingdon, J. W. (2003). *Agendas, alternatives and public policies* (2nd ed.). New York: Longman.

Klingebiel, S., & Tørres, L. (2020). Republic of Korea and COVID-19: Gleaning governance lessons from a unique approach. *Pathfinders*. UNDP. 1–10.

Kooiman, J. (2010). Chapter 5: Governance and governability. In S. P. Osborne (Ed.), *The new public governance? Emerging perspectives on the theory and practice of public governance*. New York: Routledge.

Korean Research Institute. (2020, November 25). Public opinion: 20th awareness survey related to COVID-19 (week 2, November). *Weekly Report*, *105*(2).

Kornhauser, L. A. (2004). Governance structures, legal systems, and the concept of law. *Chicago-Kent Law Review*, *79*(2), 355–381.

Kwon, S. H. (2019, November 14). The Korean's trust to their government 39% 22nd among 36 OECD member countries (in Korean). *Yonhap News Agency*. Retrieved from www.yna.co.kr/view/AKR20191114147100004

Kwon, S. S. (2016, June 2). How has Korean familism been changed? (In Korean). *Review Archive*. Retrieved from www.bookpot.net/news/articlePrint.html?idxno=779

Kwon, Y. H. (2013). Socio-philosophical examination of Korean familism (in Korean). *Society and Philosophy*, *25*, 203–232.

Kwon, Y. H. (2013a). Public and private areas: Centered on Korean modern families (in Korean). *Society and Philosophy*, *26*, 159–184.

Kye, B., & Hwang, S. J. (2020). Social trust in the midst of pandemic crisis: Implications from COVID-19 of South Korea. *Research in Social Stratification and Mobility*, *68*, 1–5.

Lancaster, K., Rhodes, T., & Rosengarten, M. (2020). Making evidence and policy in public health emergencies: Lessons from COVID-19 for adaptive evidence-making and intervention. *Evidence and Policy*, *16*(3), 477–490.

Lee, D. H. (2020, May 16). *Korean's view of state: Around 1948*. A Paper presented at the Spring Conference of the Research Society of the Korean Public Administration History (in Korean). Seminar Room of the Korean Association for Public Administration.

Lee, H. W. (2002). *Is Korea a refugee camp?* (In Korean). Seoul: Book World.

Lee, S. H. (2002). Korean people, oriental perceptions on public and private arenas and modern transformation (in Korean). *Political Philosophy Research*, *6*.

Lee, S. Y. (2020, November 25). Public opinion in public opinion: 20th perception survey on COVID-19(week 2, November) (in Korean). *Weekly Report of Korean Research Institute* (No. 105–2).

Lee, Y. W. (2020, November 3). [Science cafe] infection rate of COVID-19, South Korea is the lowest in the world. Young researchers published the results of fact-finding research on 45 nations' infections and deaths in nature (in Korean). *Chosun Daily News Paper*.

Lewis, W. A. (1965). *Politics in West Africa*. New York: Oxford University Press.

Lim, H. B. (2020, July 6). *Changes in socioeconomic order after COVID-19 pandemic (in Korean)*. A Keynote Paper presented at the Inaugural Seminar of the

Infectious Disease Research Society Organized by the National Research Council for Economics, Humanities and Social Sciences, El Tower, Seoul.
Lim, S. H. (2020, December 11). Crisis of South Korea, the world's most success model – a singular point noted by foreign press (in Korean). *Ohmynews*.
Maharaj, R. (2009). Corporate governance decision-making model: How to nominate skilled board members, by addressing the formal and informal systems. *International Journal of Disclosure and Governance*, *6*(2), 106–126.
Maruyama, M. (1995). Translated by Kim Seok-geun. In *Research on History of Japanese Political Philosophy*" (in Korean). Seoul: Tongnamoo.
Moon, M. J. (2020). Fighting COVID-19 with agility, transparency and participation: Wicked policy problems and new governance challenges. *Public Administration Review*, *80*(4), 651–656.
Moon, M. J. (2020a). COVID-19 challenges and government responses: Challenges and opportunities (in Korean). *Administrative Focus*, *147*, 41–48.
Morgenthau, H. J. (1962). Chapter 29: The corruption of patriotism. In *Politics in the twentieth century, volume 1. The decline of democratic politics*. Chicago, IL: University of Chicago Press.
Nam, S. H. (2020, September 18). Forbes, Korea is 3rd safest country (in Korean). *Korea Disaster News*. Retrieved from www.hjnews.co.kr/news/articleView.html?idxno=3000
No, H. I. (2020). COVID-19 and proactive administration (in Korean). *Administrative Focus*, *147*, 32–35.
OECD. (2013). Contextual factors influencing governance in Colombia. In *OECD, Colombia: Implementing Good Governance*. Paris, France: OECD Publishing. doi:10.1787/9789264202177-4-en
Park, H. J., & Ju, C. Y. (2020). *Korean's perceptual change of government vision, Government role and government trust (in Korean)*. EAI working paper.
Park, J. C. (2018). *Korean Governance* (in Korean). Seoul: Hankuk University of Foreign Studies Knowledge Press.
Park, K. G., & Kim, J. I. (2020). Government's role and civic culture in the post-corona era (in Korean). *Korean Public Administration Review*, *54*(3), 1–30.
Park, K. S. (2020). Lessons from COID-19 and role of government (in Korean). *Administrative Focus*, *147*, 36–40.
Park, T. H. (2004). Split and empirical review of familism concepts: Familism, egoistic familism, Pseudo-familism (in Korean). *Family and Culture*, *16*(2), 93–125.
Park, Y. I. (1985). Industrialization and familism. Korea Institute of spiritual culture (in Korean). *Spiritual Culture Research*, *8*(1).
Putnam, R. D. (1995, Spring). Bowling alone, revisited. *The Responsive Community*, 18–33.
Rogin, J. (2020, March 11). South Korea shows that democracies can succeed against the coronavirus. *Washington Post*.
Rushton, S. (2011). Global health security: Security for whom? Security from what? *Political Studies*, *59*(4), 779–796.
Shin, D. H. (2020, December 2). Reactivated residential treatment center, surpassing operating rate of 60% with 16 places (in Korean). *Medifo News*.

References

So, J. K. (2020). The importance of decentralization seen from the Korean cases of prevention and control of pandemics (in Korean). *Administrative Focus, 147*, 55–60.

Son, J. S. (2020, April 29) Guy Sorman of France, "Korea, a society that has succeeded in the quarantine but is very much monitored" (in Korean). *Chosun Daily News Paper.*

Sung, S. D. (2020, May 16). *Korean's view of state: As of 2020 (in Korean)*. A Paper presented at the Spring Conference of the Research Society of the Korean Public Administration History, Seminar Room of the Korean Association for Public Administration.

Takahashi, T. (2010). Translated by Koo In-mo. In *Discussing Koreans in colonial period* (in Korean). Seoul: Donkuk University Press.

Țicla'u, T., Hintea, C., & Andrianu, B. (2020). Adaptive and turbulent governance. Ways of governing that foster resilience: The case of the COVID-19 pandemic. *Transylvanian Review of Administrative Sciences*, Special Issue, 167–182.

van de Pas, R. (2020). Globalization paradox and the Coronavirus pandemic. In *Clingendael report*. The Hague: Netherlands Institute of International Relations.

Wee, E. J. (2020, August). Rapid test. Innovative screening center – contributed to the control of COVID-19 spread (in Korean). *Nara Economy, 357*, 10–11.

Yang, K. (2020). What can COVID-19 tell us about evidence-based management? *American Review of Public Administration, 50*(6–7), 706–712.

Zainon, S., Atan, R., Yahaya, N., & Hashim, M. (2013). Into insights of contextual governance framework for religious non-profit organizations. *International Journal of Economics and Management Engineering, 7*(12).

Zohlnhöfer, R., & Rüb, F. W. (2016). Chapter one introduction: Policy-making under ambiguity and time constraints. In R. Zohlnhöfer & F. W. Rüb (Eds.), *Decision-making under ambiguity and time constraints: Assessing the multiple-streams framework*. Colchester: ECPR Press.

Index

adaptive governance 7, 8, 53
administrative guidance 15, 27
administrative state 25, 27, 54–6
agile governance 7, 8, 53
Asian values 2, 3
authoritarian meritocracy 2
auto-administrative state 27
autonomous governance 13, 31

balanced governance 12
bottom-up implementation 10

clan family 19–21
coercive implementation 10
co-governance 12
consensual implementation 10
contextual governance 44, 46, 52, 62
contract state 24, 27, 31, 32, 37, 38, 42, 45–51, 53, 54
conversion costs 10, 43, 44, 53
cooperative governance 12, 30, 31, 34, 42–44, 47, 60
countryside aristocrats (鄉村士族) 19
cultural approach 46

defensive governance 12
deficient state 17, 51
democratic civility 43
developmental cooperatism 15
disaster diplomacy 5
disinfection capitalism 5
drive-throughs 33, 38
dual state 19, 25, 46, 47, 54, 55

echo chamber effect 37
egoistic familism 22–4, 28, 61

emotional familism 21–6, 28, 33, 35, 44
evidence-based approach 25
exclusive familism 21, 22, 24, 26, 27, 35–7, 44

familism 15, 19, 21–8, 33–7, 44, 45, 48, 53, 58–61
family state 24–7, 31–3, 35, 37, 38, 41–3, 45–8, 50, 53, 54
feedback governance 54
flat state 14, 32, 38, 42, 43, 45, 48, 49, 53, 56
forced nuclear family 20
4-T 33, 38, 48, 49
frozen state 18, 51

gentry class (兩班) 19
group extremization phenomenon 37
Garbage Can Model 8, 58
GCM *see* Garbage Can Model

hierarchical governance 12
house hold system 20
hybrid dual state 46, 47

imperial presidential system 16
implementation governance 4, 8, 11, 12, 29, 31, 42, 48, 53

June Uprising in 1987 16

laissez-faire governance 12, 13, 31
liquid society 48
low-trust society 19, 44

medical capitalism 5
mentality of system justification 37
meritocracy 2, 37
mobilization governance 12
most differential treatment 36
most favored treatment 16
multiple streams framework 9, 30, 62
MSF *see* multiple streams framework

National Debt Redemption Movement 26
needy state 17, 51
Neo-Confucianism 16, 23, 24
Neoliberalism 49, 50
non-implementation 10

open walk-throughs 38

passive governance 12, 13, 31, 37, 41–3, 47
penetration power of the state 19, 27, 38, 56
policy stream 9
politics stream 9, 10
proactive governance 13, 31, 33, 42, 43, 45, 47, 48
psychological decompression sickness symptoms 18
populism 12, 16

residential treatment center 33, 40, 61
resilient governance 7, 8, 53

scope of the state 14, 16
securitization of health 5

self-governance 13
self-governing state 26
simultaneity of the non-simultaneous 47, 65
social capital 42–4, 58
social distancing 5, 6, 33, 34, 36, 37, 44
solid society 48
stream of choices 8
stream of energy 9
stream of problems 8, 12
stream of solutions 8
switching state 25, 27, 32, 43–8
switching dual state 46

test 33, 38, 48, 62
trace 33, 39, 48
traditional familism 21, 24, 25, 27, 45
transboundary nature 4, 5
treatment 33, 36, 40, 48
trust 2, 10–4, 19, 26, 28, 32, 33, 35, 38, 40–5, 48, 53, 54, 57, 58, 60, 61
trust deficit 45, 53

vetocracy 23
vulnerable state 17, 18, 45, 51

walk-throughs 33, 38
wartime culture 25, 40
Western culture supremacy complex 55
whole-of-society approach 10

year-87 system 16, 18, 27